I0475083

Reminiscences of a Stock Market Flea™

Books by

JAMES J HOUTS

Spirit of Error

Carnival of Cannibals

The Stock Market Flea™: Trading the Crash of 2008

This book is intended for entertainment and historical purposes only. No stock market advice, stock recommendations, or broker/dealer recommendations are intended or implied. The strategies detailed are the author's and may not be suitable for anyone else. Each investor should speak with a professional investment consultant before investing. All the author's reminiscences are from his life, but the characters are fictional, any resemblance to actual people, living or dead is purely coincidental. Images not created by the author were provided by Corbis Images.

Copyright © 2013 by James J Houts
All rights reserved

Cheyenne Spring Publishing
1740H Del Range Blvd., Suite 130
Cheyenne, Wyoming 82009
USA

Library of Congress Cataloging-in-Publication Data

Houts, James J.
Reminiscences of a Stock Market Flea™ / James J. Houts

ISBN 13: 9781466430792
ISBN 10: 1466430796

Julie

for the little I know of art, music, and style.

Reminiscences of a Stock Market Flea™

James J Houts

A Movie Lover's Guide to Saving, Trading and Retirement

In the stock market there are bulls and there are bears.

One or the other is always in the lead.

I just want to be a flea—

small, nimble, and ready to hop from one to the other for a tiny bite.

Reminiscences of a Stock Market Flea™

Contents

List of Movies

There is a tide in the affairs of men.
Which, taken at the flood, leads on to fortune;
Omitted, all the voyage of their life is bound in
shallows and in miseries.
On such a full sea are we now afloat,
And we must take the current when it serves,
Or lose our ventures.

William Shakespeare

Overture

Action!

How I Beat the S&P Average by 56 Percent in 2008

In the 1962 movie *Lonely are the Brave*, Kirk Douglas stars as Jack Burns, a cowboy who won't accept the changes of the modern-day world. George Kennedy plays the mean jail guard, Deputy Gutierrez. Burns protects his friend Paul Bond, played by Michael Kane, from the sadistic Gutierrez, and the jailer turns his hate to him. When Gutierrez demands his name, Burns says happily, "John W. Burns." That night Gutierrez calls his name menacingly from the far off entrance to the cellblock, "John...W...Burns." In his cell, Burns starts preparing for the beating he knows he is going to get, tearing small pieces from his shirt, and stuffing them up his nose and under his lip. When his cellmate asks him what the hell he's doing, Burns replies calmly between bites of his shirt, "Nose of mine cracks easy. Man's going to give me fair notice, no reason I shouldn't prop it up a little."

***

I have been investing in the stock market for thirty-five years and in the real estate market for twenty-five. In 2008, when almost every other investor got crushed, and even the Wall Street "experts" were down by almost half, I was up 17 percent—beating the S&P Average by over 50 percent. I made some good trades during 2008, but most of that 50 percent "beat" was made before the stock and real estate markets rolled over. I did it by seeing the danger coming and taking steps to protect myself—you might say I stuffed a little of my shirt up under my lip. This book is the story of how I did it and how you too can do it in the future.

I spent most of the 1990s outside North America, working as an expatriate for a major specialty chemicals company. When I was repatriated, just before the turn of the millennium, I realized that being away so long had dramatically slowed the normal accumulation of wealth needed for a comfortable retirement. I was way behind in my plan and had to catch up in a hurry. *Anybody out there familiar with that feeling?* I dedicated my life to my engineering career and my investment plan. By the time the crash picked up momentum in November 2007, I had funded my retirement, retired from my engineering job, and I was day-trading full time. I was blind to the fact that seven years of total commitment to corporate life had distorted my view of that world and the value of wealth and power.

During the years between 2000 and 2006 I made huge gains in the final, frothy stages of the real estate market. I also booked big gains in the final leg up of the decades-long bull market on Wall Street—the bull market that came to a screeching end in November 2007. Yes, I took a big hit, along with almost everyone else, when the dot-com bubble burst in 2001, but I was able to recover my losses and much more. In fact, I was hit particularly hard by the dot-com bubble because I had been unable to trade for years while living overseas and foolishly tried to make up for lost time once I got back—betting the farm just before the bubble burst. But the dot-com bubble taught me a very valuable, if expensive, lesson: *You don't want to be the last one out.*

By the end of 2005, most of the experts were wondering if there was a real estate bubble and the stock market bull was looking very long in the tooth too. I could hear the terrifying voice of George Kennedy calling to me from the darkness: *John...W...Burns.* In August 2006 I sold my last piece of real estate. I began selling my property in December 2003, so I didn't optimize my profits during the last, hyperbolic move in the real estate boom, but I did book better than 100 percent returns based on buy and sell prices—returns that were dwarfed by actual, after-tax profits made through the everyday use of mortgage leverage. My profit, on a duplex in Manhattan Beach, California, was almost twenty times my initial investment after just four years. I have included a detailed explanation of how leverage can be a very good thing in chapter 8, "Real Estate," and how leverage can be a very dangerous thing in chapter 10, "What Happened to the Markets?"

In early 2007, the inflation rate in China exceeded 10 percent, and I stuffed some more of my shirt up my investment nose. I had been heavily invested in China—at times more than 50 percent of my total investment portfolio—since repatriating to the United States. Being "long," China was a major part of my retirement plan. I had worked and traveled in China extensively and had witnessed the strength of the Chinese economy firsthand. I had become a believer. There were, of course, some crazy aspects of the Chinese economy too. I once watched a hundred Chinese guys digging a drainage ditch with picks and shovels in front of a Caterpillar sales yard that was packed with shiny yellow D-5 Cats. On another occasion, we waited on a mountain road as fifty guys used a capstan they had driven into the middle of the road to wind a tow truck up from a gorge below. Working in China was as entertaining as it was educational.

My given name is James, but my third grade teacher thought it a good idea to give me the nickname Jim. It stuck for a very long time. By the late 1990s, I was selling engineering services in China. I made presentations at many meetings where I was the only English speaker there. My meeting plan, which had worked many times before, was to start my presentations by introducing myself and exchanging pleasantries in my broken Chinese; I thought my potential customers would appreciate my effort. I was just beginning to learn Mandarin, so I always had a local Chinese translator with me, although I worked with some who didn't know an apple from an atom.

Before one presentation I got lucky and hired a local translator who was fluent not only in English but also in chemical engineering. She was very smart, but almost incapacitated by her shyness. As the meeting got started, I introduced myself per my call plan, but to my surprise a quiet twitter rustled among the men seated at the board table, contorting their upturned faces with muffled giggles and suppressed grins. These were serious men and our meeting was to discuss serious money. My Chinese clients were almost always stoically bland; I was stunned by the out-break of stifled laughter.

After the meeting and the obligatory exchange of gifts, I finally got my translator alone—I was dying to know what I had done to screw up the meeting. For my young and shy translator it was worse than a root canal to tell me what had happened, but I insisted. Then finally, with her chin on her chest and her eyes on the ground she said, "In this city's local dialect, 'jim' sounds a lot like the slang word for a woman's private parts. They found it funny when you introduced yourself as Jim." *Oh, crap!*

That night I called my office in Shanghai and had the secretary order me some new business cards—printed with James instead of Jim. I never went by Jim again.

> **Lesson:** *When your plan gets trumped by the facts—change the plan.*

I saw the high inflation rate in China as a sign of bad things to come and liquidated all my stock-market-based positions to cash in March 2007. Within a week, the Shanghai stock market dropped by 9 percent in a single night and I was patting myself on the back for getting out before the market correction I had been expecting got traction.

But the China markets roared back after the March slump, as did the US markets. I had sold out early and missed much of the big gains in the stock market during the six months between March and October; as you read on, you will learn that I am usually early, what I call a jackrabbit, and it has sometimes cost me a lot of money. But in late 2007, when the markets became money-devouring monsters, I was positioned overwhelmingly in cash. I was convinced that there was an imminent decline lurking and I maintained my high cash position through the end of the year, although I didn't have any idea of the magnitude of the coming crash.

I did do very well in my options trading in the months leading up to the disaster. I was up over 30 percent in my small high-frequency trading account, though these gains were crushed during the first leg down of the bear market in November and December 2007. In 2008 I traded options in my high-frequency account to increase my net worth by 17 percent while risking only 10–15 percent of my worth at any one time; 2008 was the year almost everyone else took a 50 percent hit. All in, I beat the S&P Index by about 56 percent in 2008; and while real estate prices were in free fall I was a happy renter.

The 1967 movie classic *Cool Hand Luke*, directed by Stuart Rosenberg, starred Paul Newman and George Kennedy. Newman plays Luke, an antiestablishment prisoner in a very scary Florida prison camp. While playing poker with the other prisoners, led by Kennedy's tough-guy character, Dragline, Luke wins the hand by bluffing. When Dragline sees his hand he exclaims, "But you had nothing!" Luke responds coolly—Newman was always very cool—"Yeah, well…sometimes nothing can be a real cool hand."

So when the real estate market melted down and the stock market went south, the hand I was holding was nothing, but it was "a real cool hand."

I wrote this book by accident. After spending half of 2007 in cash, watching the markets go up while I waited for them to break, the weak signal finally arrived. I had continued to chart the daily progress of the US mutual funds I had sold in March (growth, value, mid-cap, small cap), and in October I noticed that they had stopped moving up. In fact, they had leveled off and were starting to move lower. I had also been following the international funds I had liquidated (China, India, Japan, Southeast Asia) and only the China fund continued to make new highs. It seemed that the global markets were also faltering. I documented every day, in fact every trade, in my trading log. I was fascinated by what I saw as a historic moment and I wanted to record all of my reasons for taking the positions I took and making the trades I made. My trading log and the market newsletter I started at the height of the crisis became the basis of this book.

A few months before the markets rolled over, I decided to retire from my engineering job and informed my company that I would be leaving at the end of the year. I couldn't justify working ten or twelve hours a day without passion at a job that didn't pay. My option trading in my high-frequency account was consistently earning two or three times what I was making as an engineer, and I was doing it during a few hours in the mornings and at night. My income had grown to the point that my take-home pay would be almost the same whether I worked as an engineer or not—taxes took most of the extra money. In October 2007 I spoke with my boss and told him I wouldn't be able to make it to the end of the year after all; there was a historic market break coming and I needed to spend all my time trading.

In November 2007 I made some very bad choices just when the market risk was starting to soar and I gave back a good part of the gains I had made in my high-frequency account since March—over $80,000—in a single, disastrous two-day options trade. After options expiration day, I licked my wounds and thought about a quote from one of the Indiana Jones movies.

Indiana Jones and the Last Crusade (1989) was directed by Steven Spielberg and produced by cowriter George Lucas (with Jeffrey Boam).

How is that for an A team? As always, the movie starred Harrison Ford as Indiana, but this chapter added the always-wonderful and entertaining Sean Connery as Indiana's elderly dad. Father and son go on another adventurous quest, fighting Nazis all the way, this time in search of the Holy Grail and its power to give immortality to anyone who drinks from it. After they finally find the Grail room, the evil Nazi collaborator who has dogged them the entire movie selects from the many chalices and takes a heady drink. Wrong cup. He dissolves in a gory mess; finally turning to dust, he blows away. The seven-hundred-year-old Grail Knight, played by Robert Eddison, says with great import and obvious wisdom, "He chose...poorly."

I had chosen poorly in a horrendous Goldman Sachs options trade, but the loss went a long way to convince me, by handing me my severed head, that the markets had really begun to break. I remembered a presentation CNBC's Steve Liesman had made in late 2006 or early 2007 in which he used an old-fashioned flip chart and markers to explain how the mortgage-backed-obligation (MBO) market had been engineered. He had seemed befuddled about how the market could exist and how the bonds themselves could be valued in the way they were. By the end of the first quarter of 2008 the world was beginning to realize that the MBO market was a gigantic house of cards and the credit default swaps (CDSs) the speculators (sharks) used to bet against them were the gasoline and the spark to burn it down. I did a calculation on the size of the outstanding CDS obligation and the number was terrifying—it would take the gross domestic product of the entire world over a decade to pay them off.

In 2008 I traded every day, tens of thousands of options as the markets went down and dozens and dozens of stock trades as I hoped there might be a tradable bottom. But I always kept the vast majority of my net worth in cash, risking only tiny portions at any one time, moving in and moving out quickly, and by the end of the December I had managed to have a good year. Quick and small are hallmarks of the Stock Market Flea.

Then at the end of 2008, I finally looked away from my trading computer and took inventory of the economic devastation surrounding me. I spoke to my family and friends and realized for the first time that almost everyone, including the stock market gurus on TV, had lost almost half of everything. I also realized that my trading performance had been vastly different. I had done something very few had been able to do: I had beaten the crash. At end of 2008 I was up 17 percent in the stock market for the year and I had sold out of my real estate at the market peak. When I read through my investment log I realized I had a pretty good draft for a book—this one.

When I started out trading in 1978 I didn't know much about the stock market. In fact I knew exactly zilch, but that is really the point. You don't need to know much to be a good trader and you need to know even less to protect yourself from the disasters.

This book is not one of those *Cash McCall* stories where some rich guy buys and sells companies like you and I might trade in a car. *Cash McCall* was a great 1960 movie starring James Garner and Natalie Wood. Directed by Joseph Pevney, the movie glamorizes what we now call private-equity investment. Garner's character, McCall, runs a venture-capital company, similar to Mitt Romney's Bain Capital. He bought companies on the cheap, fixed them up or broke them up, and then flipped them for big profits. And it isn't one of those books where a Wall Street insider buys a million shares of Dow Jones at forty dollars each—that'll be the day, when I, or you, lay on a trade worth forty million bucks—and doubles his money over night. I am *not* a professional trader. I didn't go to Harvard as an undergrad and I don't have a degree from Harvard Law, or the invaluable money and power contacts that go along with them, as one of my favorite TV market mavens does. I'm not an economist. I don't have a business degree, a stockbroker's license, a financial-planning certificate, or any other professional qualification to give investment advice. So I won't.

What I do have is the experience of working a day job while investing for my retirement. I use the term "day job" loosely—you can't trade options when you're working on an ammonia-plant deal in Western China or a power-plant deal in West Africa as I did in the 1990s. I worked in the corporate world as a chemist or chemical engineer for almost thirty years while investing in real estate, stocks, bonds, and options. During my almost thirty-five years of investing I have learned a few things that should be helpful to anyone who has accepted the unpleasant fact that each person's retirement is his or her own responsibility.

There is still time; I built most of the wealth I needed to retire at age fifty-three in just seven years.

Don't look for much help from your corporation or the government. They won't tell you how to save or where, which books to buy and read—and they won't show you how to trade. I'm going to try to do all three. There is a list of books written by *real* investment gurus in the bibliography in the back of this one.

The only qualification I have to write this book is my record and the history of the real estate and stock market crash of 2008:

- Real estate: The Shiller Index of real estate prices shows that between the first quarter (Q1) of 2006 and Q1 2007, the national average home price increased 12 percent. I sold my last piece of real estate in early August 2006, at the historic peak of the real estate market. I will detail many of my real estate deals in chapter 8, but I sold this last property for twenty times my original down payment and was completely out of real estate when the historic break in values hit. Between Q1 2007 and Q4 2011, real estate values crashed—down 2 percent in 2007, 14 percent in 2008, and another painful 19 percent in 2009. In 2010 there was a small recovery in home values of 2 percent that was more than erased by another 5 percent decline in 2011.

- The stock market: During 2008 my investment portfolio was up big. Although I never put much more than 10–15 percent of my net worth at risk at any one time, my net worth was up more than 17 percent at the end of the year. If I exclude paper profits made from venture-capital investments, my stock and options trading increased my net worth by 4.7 percent. During the same period the Dow Jones Industrial Average was down 34 percent, the S&P 500 Index was down 39 percent and the NASDAQ Exchange Average was down an astounding 41 percent.

So I sold the last of my real estate in August 2006 and closed out my long-term stock market positions in March 2007. That is how, after being leveraged in ocean-view real estate for twenty years and fully invested in the stock market for over thirty years, I was almost completely in cash, holding a real cool hand, when the biggest real estate and stock market crash of our time slammed the world markets. And five years later, I still have some bits of my shirt stuffed up under my upper lip.

Chapter 1

Saving

Paying Yourself First; the Joy of Deferred Gratification

In *It's a Wonderful Life*, Frank Capra's classic 1946 Christmas movie, the incomparable Jimmy Stewart plays George Bailey, the president of a family-owned savings and loan, trying to save the business during a bank run. Mr. Potter, the greedy old slumlord, is played by the great American actor of stage, screen, and radio, Lionel Barrymore. Mr. Potter says that trusting people and giving them home loans creates "a discontented, lazy rabble instead of a thrifty working class." "Take this loan to Ernie Bishop…," Potter goes on; "the bank turned down this loan, but we're building him a house worth five thousand dollars. Why?" Bailey pleads for the life of the town and its citizens, "What did you say just a minute ago? They had to wait and save their money before they even ought to think of a decent home. Wait! Wait for what?" Then Bailey asks, "Do you know how long it takes a working man to save five thousand dollars?"

***

Saving five thousand in 1946 would take about as long as saving a couple of million dollars now. After the war the government offered the returning GIs financial aid for a year; it was called "fifty-two/twenty." Twenty dollars a week for fifty-two weeks: $1,040 to live on for a year. Most of these GIs had wives and new babies, as did my dad. But my dad was a proud man, so proud he literally dug ditches for twenty bucks a week instead taking the fifty-two/twenty.

In the 1960s behavioral psychologists came up with experiments to measure the ability of preschoolers to resist temptation and defer gratification. Called impulse studies, the experiments offered the children the choice between a small reward now or a larger reward later. Walter Mischel's group at Stanford University did the seminal work creating the structure of the experiments. Children were left alone with a delicious treat (a marshmallow, a cookie, a gummy bear) but were given two options:

- They could ring a bell to bring the researcher back early and eat the single treat.

- They could wait for the researcher to return in about fifteen minutes and get two or more of the same treat.

The subjects of the studies were children, so most rang the bell and ate the single treat. More than a decade later, the researchers followed up to see how the kids did on their SAT tests. The ones who were able to wait scored much higher on their tests.

This book is about investing. To invest money, you need to have some. The definition of a capitalist is one who uses capital (money) to make more capital. So to be a capitalist—our goal—you need to have some investment capital. Unless you were born into it and have family money, or you have won the lottery, or you have special abilities or characteristics that allow you to play NBA basketball or star in block-buster movies, the sad fact is you will need to save some money to be able to invest. The good news is you don't need to be an evil Mr. Potter to get it.

I learned how to save when the banks brought little savings account books to our school every week. The passbooks were transported in tiny envelopes with string ties to keep them closed. We would put a nickel or a dime into the passbook envelope, and a bank representative would come to school to collect them. The next week the passbook would reflect the new deposit. I am a believer in saving. In fact, the advice I give to my family, friends, and partners is: Save 25 percent of your gross. If you earn $10,000 per month, you need to save $2,500. If you make $1,000 per month, you need to save $250. Here is the rub. It is much easier to save $2,500 out of $10,000 per month than $250 out of a $1,000, but who needs to save more? I followed this plan most of my life and I retired at fifty-three. Members of my family have tried to do this, without 100 percent success, and still they were much better off during the times they couldn't save and needed to dip into their savings to survive.

I include all types of saving in the 25 percent total. If you have a company sponsored 401(k) savings program at work, as I did during most of my working career, your company may have a matching program. If anyone ever offers to match your savings—*take it!* This is free money. For instance, if you have a "one to two" company match up to, say, 8 percent of your gross and you make $10,000 per month ($120,000 per year), you put in $8,000 and your company puts in $4,000 free money. You *must* take all the "free money" and the only way to do that is to save the first $8,000.

Tax-Deferred Retirement Accounts
I am a fiscal conservative. I believe government should not spend money profligately and they should minimize the amount of taxes they take out of the economic system. I also believe that it is our obligation as citizens and investors to do what is right, not only for our government but for ourselves. Taxes are a necessary evil, but I believe taxes should be minimized whenever possible. Not considering the tax liabilities of our

3

investments before we enter into them can define the difference between a comfortable retirement and a time of financial stress and money concerns when we can least afford them.

In 1974 Congress and president Gerald Ford created the Employee Retirement Income Security Act; a small almost unnoticed section created the individual retirement account, the IRA. For the first time, you were allowed to defer taxes on earned income if you put it into a separate account, which would incur huge penalties if the money was removed before retirement age. It was almost unused, however, because you were only eligible if you had no company retirement plan, and in those days most people still had them. Then in 1982, Congress made the IRA *universal* by expanding the program to anyone under 70-½ years old, even if they did have a corporate retirement plan. The limit was $2,000 per year.

So I had an idea. In the early 1980s, *all* interest was still tax deductible, even the interest on your car loan. So I went to my credit union and borrowed $2,000 at the lowest interest rate I could get, drove over to Charles Schwab, and opened a new IRA with the money. Talk about gaming the income tax law at both ends—I was able to deduct from my income taxes both the $2,000 I put into the IRA and the interest I paid on the loan. It was a great edge while it lasted, but the interest rate deduction was soon limited to real estate. Since those early days, my IRA, which I funded every year, has more than tripled—it was up four fold until I got caught long BP (formally British Petroleum) during the Macondo blowout in the Gulf of Mexico in 2010. I will go into this nightmarish trade gone wrong in agonizing detail—for me, anyway—later in this book.

In a 401(k) you won't need to pay taxes on the money until you take it out. While living in Hawaii during the 1990s, I dated a woman who managed a small brokerage office in Honolulu. We had heated debates about whether deferred taxation was a smart thing to take or not. If this book was about relationship advice, I would advise young bachelors to *not* have heated debates with their girlfriends. Remember what happened to Michael Douglas and Kathleen Turner in the 1989 Movie,

The War of the Roses? Danny DeVito directed and starred in this dark comedy that takes a happy couple down the bitter path of divorce. Not a very happy ending.

As a stockbroker, my girlfriend had been thoroughly indoctrinated into thinking it was always the smart move to fund an IRA or 401(k). My point was that 401(k) money is *not* tax free; it is tax deferred. That means you don't pay taxes now, but you do pay the taxes when you take it out—both on the gains you have made and the original pay-roll taxes you have waited to pay. You will pay taxes when you take the money out, at whatever the future income tax rate is at the time. You will pay this rate—currently the maximum income tax rate is 35 percent—not only on the income you deferred paying taxes on initially, but also on whatever capital gains you earned on the money while it was in the 401(k). Currently the capital gains tax rate is 15 percent, so if you become wealthy during your lifetime and wind up paying the maximum income tax rate when you take the money out, you will pay 20 percent more on the capital gains made on the money in the deferred account than if you had made the same gains outside of the account. Putting your savings in a 401(k) account and deferring the income tax on current earnings is a good thing based on the following assumptions:

1. You will be in the same or lower tax bracket when you take the money out.

2. The compounding of returns made inside the 401(k) will compensate for what could be a 20 percent higher tax rate when you start withdrawals.

3. You are, so the government thinks, without the discipline to save without its helpful incentives.

The assumption is that when you retire you will be poorer than during your working career; but if you win the lottery, inherit a lot of money, become wealthy on your own brains and sweat; become a movie star, or publish a best seller later in life—or if you have just managed, against all odds, to save up a nest egg—you may wind up paying more taxes than if you had taken the money and paid the tax originally. And if the government increases the income tax rate (*no, they would never do that*), the result could be that that you will have a much larger tax bill, as income tax, when you are *required* to take the money out than you would have had as capital gains tax each year along the way. Currently the law requires you begin to take the money out when you are 70-½. You can begin taking it at 59-½.

A Roth IRA may be a better bet if you expect this outcome. With a Roth IRA you pay the income taxes on the money before it goes in. It is best to seek advice from a good tax accountant for your personal situation.

But even though I believed the broker tout for retirement accounts might be wrong, I *still* put the maximum amounts into all my 401(k) accounts, beyond the amounts the companies matched. In the case of one company that would match up to 8 percent, I could still put in, by law, up to 12 percent of my gross earnings. There was also a dollar limit, but in those days I was far under it. In 2012 the limit is $17,000 per year, but it wasn't this way when I got started; the limits were lower. Today, for people closer to retirement, there is also a so-called catch-up limit that allows an additional $5,500 contribution, for a total of $22,500. I also kept putting money into my IRA, outside of the corporate 401(k) programs. In 1982 the IRA originally had a limit of $2,000 per year, but it too has grown larger. In 2012 the limit is $5,000 with a catch-up provision that brings it up to $6,000.

It seemed to me that even though the brokerage-house mantra was not completely true, and I might wind up paying higher taxes in the end, it still made sense that the first money I saved would be tax deferred. I will never win the lottery. I know this because I don't buy lottery tickets. Saving this way first is especially smart if you get matching money. I understand that this can be difficult, but if your company is willing to match half of the money you put in, you *must* take it, regardless of the pain.

As an example, let's use the 2012 limits for a person who has not reached the minimum age of 50-½ for the catch-up provision. The taxpayer earns $120,000 per year and has saved $8,000 in the 401(k), plus $4,000 (free money), plus another $5,000 in the 401(k) that is not matched, for a total of $17,000. Our hypothetical taxpayer also puts the maximum of $5,000 into an IRA account for a grand total of $22,000, or 18.3 percent of the earned gross. This is the first 18 percent this earner needs to save. There is still 7 percent left to save (based on my rule of saving 25 percent), and this is the money I would use for riskier stock market trading outside of tax deferred accounts.

Where an investment is made, the account structure within which the trade is executed, can make all of the difference between a good profit and an after tax loss. Should riskier trades be made inside a tax-deferred account or outside in a conventional cash account? One stockbroker I worked with for years believed that the risky stuff should be done within tax-deferred accounts. But you can't deduct wins against losses inside a 401(k) as you can in a cash account. I listened, but didn't follow his advice on this one. On one occasion this broker had invited me to play golf at Donald Trump's course on the Palos Verdes peninsula in Los Angeles. His firm had a big push on to move their clients into government bonds, so they were getting their big spenders out for golf to sell it. Remember, a stockbroker is a salesman who wants your money; he is not your golfing buddy. The only reason I was getting the free golf was I had spent tens of thousands of dollars in options commissions with him during the year.

The big problem some people have about the tax-deferred retirement accounts (IRAs and 401Ks) is the huge penalty for early withdrawal. It really stings if you do it, which is exactly why they were built that way—to incentivize you to leave the money alone and let it grow. But I have figured out a way to synthetically take the money out. I call it "black hole evaporation."

Although nothing can ever get free of a black hole (hence the name), Stephen Hawking tells us that black holes eventually dissipate through the process of quantum mechanical evaporation—a phenomenon wherein subatomic particles simply wink out of existence inside the black hole and then reappear elsewhere in the universe. Over time—lots of it—the black hole just goes away.

Here is my black hole evaporation method of taking liquidity from retirement accounts—401Ks and IRAs—without paying taxes or penalties while lowering the tax liability when withdrawals begin.

- Buy a very high alpha and high beta stock (high risk, high opportunity) in a retirement account.

- Then, in a conventional cash account, outside the retirement account, buy the option protection on the risky trade. There will be more about options in chapter 5.

If the stock in the retirement account goes up big, the profits are protected inside and taxed at the retirement account rates when taken out later. The cash account option protection bought outside the retirement account will decrease toward zero in this happy case; the losses can be used against taxable gains. But if the stock in the retirement account takes a dump, the option protection bought outside the controlled account will soar—and at a faster rate because of the option leverage.

So if the stock goes up, the retirement account goes up and the option losses are deductible from current trading income. If the stock goes down, the amount paid in taxes, when disbursements from the account begin, is much smaller, while the taxes on the options profits are paid outside the retirement account on a yearly basis—while you still have a job. If the stocks purchased in the retirement account are consistently losers, the options traded as a hedge outside the account will more than compensate for the losses due to the inherent leverage of options. The net effect of this trade is a gradual reduction of the amount of money in the retirement account and an increase in the amount of money outside. The money in the retirement account has evaporated and recondensed outside the legal structure of the retirement account that penalizes early withdrawals.

Recently I found out that owning a master limited partnership (MLP) within a 401(k) or an IRA can be a nightmare. MLPs are very attractive because they pay out all of their earnings as dividends. You are actually a partner in the company and share all the profits. They are also attractive because all of the partnership's expenses are deducted from the earnings dividends paid so the taxes are rarely severe. I knew that owning these very high-dividend payers would be a tax accounting headache so I bought them in my 401(k) account. After all, you only pay taxes on a 401(k) when you take the money out, right? Wrong. And I even checked with my accountant on this before doing it. He was oblivious to the actual tax liability.

Here is what really happens. The MLP sends you a K-1, technically a form 1065 (Schedule K-1) but the two accountants, three stockbrokers, and two IRS representatives I spoke with about the form all simply use the term K-1. The K-1 itemizes the MLP's expenses. You need to use this information to fill out an IRS form 990-T to claim unrelated business income and submit it to the IRS. If taxes are required, the taxes need to be paid from the 401(k) in which the MLP was owned. *Is this getting complicated enough for you?* And since the brokerage house in which the 401(k) is held is the legal custodian of the 401(k), it is they who need to file the 990-T and pay the taxes—out of your account, of course.

My oblivious accountant actually argued with me about this, and he is a good one. I had to provide him with Internet links to educate him. Then he said he still didn't know how to do it and that I would need to fill out the 990-T myself. *Here is your bill. Thanks a lot!*

So I went to the brokerage houses where I do business. Here is how that went:

- TD Ameritrade said I was on my own. I should fill out the 990-T (their job) and send it in. They would forward it on to the IRS.

- Scottrade was ignorant of the law, thinking (as I had, originally) that you only pay taxes on a 401(k) when you take money out.

- Charles Schwab said, "Send us the K-1. We will fill out the 990-T and file the paperwork with the IRS. We will send you copies for your files."

I am currently in the process of moving all my retirement accounts to Charles Schwab. They have the best tax department of any of them. They even spent several hours on a conference call with my accountant and me to help sort out the tax liability of a venture capital position I had held in one of their accounts. They did this for free; my oblivious accountant sent me a bill for $750. They are the best choice of the three brokers I have been using for years. I am also looking for an accountant who does more stock market and corporate-related tax preparations.

But in the defense of the oblivious accountant and the ignorant and unhelpful brokerage houses, the IRS wasn't much better. When I couldn't figure out how to fill out the 990-T, I called the IRS. The person I got had never heard of a 990-T and said that he would find someone to call me back. The call back came in about two weeks, just before the filing deadline. The guy who called me wanted to get into detail immediately, but not surprisingly, I didn't have all my documents in front of me. There was no way I could work on the stuff driving a car with a cell phone in one hand and my records in a file cabinet at home. He finally said, and I quote, "Well, the amounts you are talking about are small, so it probably won't matter."

Not until they yank me in for an audit, it won't. Geez!

There was an investment guru named Raymond Lucia who was very popular before the crash. In his book *Buckets of Money* he recommended buckets for different kinds of investments. Each bucket did something different: one was for the low-yield, low-risk money you absolutely didn't want to lose; another was for the high-risk, high-return money that allowed you to beat inflation. He had other buckets and ideas that you should get from his books, which are listed in my bibliography. I liked what he said, but just as I was trying to put his plan into play, the investment world came apart. However, when I look back at how I have invested for the past thirty-five years, I have done it in much the way he recommended. My investments were—if not deliberately in separate buckets—separated into safe and not-so-safe strategies. My safe money was always the money in the tax deferred 401(k) accounts. I did originally use my first IRA money in risky investments, but that was a different time, before the 401(k) program came into being.

I read an article recently that had been written by the senior VP of equity ratings for a huge brokerage house. He said, "Historically, US government bonds have been a relatively safe investment, but again, we can't say that they always will be, only that they should be."

Yep, put your hard-earned money in Treasuries at the peak of the market, you can always let the bonds go to term and earn the 1.5 percent interest rate forever.

I can tell you one thing, with historically low interest on these bonds, which means historically high prices, they have very little potential for appreciation and huge potential to cost you a bundle when interest rates go up. Personally, I'm waiting for double-digit rates with low prices before I buy Treasuries. This happened in the late 1970s and early 1980s when, like now, we had an unfunded war debt to inflate away. But then, my job is not to sell bonds—regardless of what they will do to the buyer's wallet. He goes on to say, "Saving 2 percent more of your income…can be a much more certain way to build retirement wealth than investing more aggressively to earn potentially 2 percent higher returns." There is much more about Treasury bonds in chapter 6.

He is right about one thing: save more. But don't save stupidly. A 0.8 percent money-market rate with almost zero risk is better than a 1.5 percent Treasury with the real risk of losing half of your investment if rates skyrocket up. There is risk of inflation diminishing your buying power if you stay in cash, but you have that risk in low-rate, high-cost government bonds too.

My father was a mechanic. Each year our "tax man" would come to the house and do Dad's taxes. In 1970 he was surprised to see that Dad's income had risen to $20,000 per year. Dad was a good provider for his family, but we really didn't have many of the extras. I seem now to have become much wealthier than Dad ever was.

In 1970, before president Richard Nixon took us off the gold standard, the price of gold was $32 per ounce. The Nixon administration's move to a fiat currency is at the root of our current crisis, but poor decisions were the hallmark of that administration. Nixon's choice for treasury secretary, a critical job during those treacherous times, was John Connally, who had absolutely *no* economic training. He would later declare personal bankruptcy—incredible for a guy who once ran our treasury. In 2011, forty years after Nixon and Connolly took us off the gold standard, the price of gold reached about $1,800 per ounce. In today's dollars, in terms of a McDonald's Big Mack, which was $0.50 in 1971 and is $4.33 in mid-2012, after an 866 percent devaluation in the buying power of the US dollar, my dad's $20,000 per year would be $173,000 in today's money. In terms of gold or real buying power, my dad's $20,000 is equal to $1.1 million per year. I don't feel nearly so rich when I think of it that way.

Safe Retirement Income-Using Options—Outside Tax-Deferred Accounts
When I started writing this book, all I wanted to write about was the options market; I have written and stated repeatedly that if an investor doesn't understand options, they should not be investing in individual stocks. That is analogous to buying a house and not procuring fire insurance. If you compare the relative values of the Dow and S&P stock indexes in 1999 and in 2011, you will find very little net change; despite the sickening rollercoaster ride during the period, the markets have gone nowhere fast. In fact, the value of the NASDAQ composite is significantly lower. If you had only been invested in stocks during those dozen years, without option protection, your wallet is probably a whole lot lighter today than it should be. The big

dogs (food for us fleas)—the bulls and the bears—never think about an individual stock without considering how owning that stock might affect the overall risks and returns of their entire investment portfolio. As fleas, we want to imitate this investment behavior; we understand that there are risks to investing, and that not being invested has its own kind of risk, but we also need to know how to insure ourselves against that risk.

We can think of stock options in terms of real estate. Lately, I have been shopping to buy a house. If, however, I believe that housing has more downside to come, I might enter into a "lease with an option to buy" agreement with a seller. Let's say the owner wants $500,000 for the house. We might agree that I lease the house for $2,000 per month for one year, with all the normal stipulations of a lease agreement (a contract), but with an additional option that I can choose to buy the house at the seller's price ($500K) any time during the lease term (one year). We sign the contract in July 2012. The seller makes $24,000 in rent during the year (the time premium) and I get to lock in the price of the house (the strike price). If by the end of the year, the value of the house is above the $500K strike price there would be intrinsic value. If the house price increased to $550,000 and I had a contract to buy it at $500,000, the intrinsic value of the contract would be $50,000. I would exercise the contract and buy the house at the agreed upon $500K. If the house value is way below the $500K strike price, the intrinsic value would be zero and I would not exercise the option to buy. Whether or not I exercise the option to buy, I am out the $24,000 in rent I have paid. The rent I've been paying (the time premium) has allowed me to keep my options open. This is how a call option works. In stock-option terms, this example would be the June 2013 call option with a strike price of $500,000 and a premium of $24,000.

I spend a lot of time explaining the options market in chapter 5: the types of option contracts and how they are routinely utilized by both bulls and bears to make huge returns while protecting their principal.

But I am going to show one example here because options can, and should, also be used to optimize returns on boring stocks that pay dividends.

Take any stock with a dividend and a little volatility. By "volatility" I mean that the stock moves up and down enough that the option prices have a significant amount of time premium—what I call "the spice" (much more about that later). Higher spice is a good thing when you are selling options and an additional cost when you are buying them. But for investors who are looking to add income to their account, higher spice will help. Let's take Intel as an example.

I prefer trading the options of Apple because the option market around Apple stock is very deep; there are many, many contracts with strikes every $5, expiration dates almost every month, and a huge turnover. This liquidity gives me plenty of directions to play Apple, and I have confidence that I can sell out of a position when I need or want to get out—two very different motivations for a trader. But with Apple stock selling at over $600, a thousand shares of Apple will set you back the hefty sum of $600,000. Ouch! But a thousand shares of Intel, which has much lower volatility and therefore lower spice, will only set you back about $25,000—a lot, but a more manageable amount if you are small like a flea. And since Intel has a huge number of shares outstanding—a big float—and millions of shares traded every day, Intel also has a very deep options market.

So, for our example, I arbitrarily selected a date in mid-July 2012 and found the following:

- Intel common stock traded at $25.13, with a quarterly dividend of $0.21 or 3.34 percent. I like this company and want to own it (again) and have a buy target of $25.

- Intel October 2012 $24 put option is trading at $0.90.

Perfect. I want to sell the puts. *Uh-oh, this sounds dangerous—and it is, sort of.*

The Downside

Normally, I avoid selling naked puts. You will learn much more about the bad things that can happen to you when you sell naked puts when you read the discussion in chapter 5 about my painful BP (formally British Petroleum) trade. The important thing is that when you sell a put contract you are required to buy the stock at the contract price on the contract date. If I sell the puts above—no matter what happens, I keep the $0.90—I will be required to buy Intel on October 20, 2012, for $24. Alternatively, I can buy back the puts at the going rate anytime between the time I sold them and their expiration date—the third Friday in October. The catch, of course, is that if the stock goes down hugely, as it did in my BP trade, and I don't buy back the puts quickly, I have $24 of downside. That is, if the stock goes to $1, the puts will increase in value to somewhere in the vicinity of $23. So if I wait until then to buy back the puts, I will lose $23 less the premium I received of $0.90 or $22.10 on each share. *And that will leave a mark.* If I don't buy back the puts, I will buy the now $1 stock at $24. Leaving me a $23.10 loss.

But, hold on a minute! I wanted to buy Intel as soon as it hit $25 anyway. If I bought the stock, I would still have the downside, but without the $0.90 in my pocket. If I sell the put contract, and it is *exercised* at $24, I have bought the stock at $24 - $0.90, or $23.10. That is $1.90 less than my target price. *What is wrong with that?*

So, if Intel is at $24 on October 20, I will own the stock I want now at $25, but at a 7.6 percent discount to my target price. *Hmm, this isn't so dangerous, is it?* I do need to set a stop-loss point or buy-back target before I enter the trade—this is the most important part of minimizing losses— whether I sell a put or if I buy a stock outright. This is the essential part of trading I allowed my emotions negate in my disastrous BP trade.

When I select a buy-back target for puts, or a stop-loss sell point for a stock, I ask myself, "How much am I willing to lose before I want out?" In the example above, I might select 5 percent, based on the contracted stock buy price of $24. 5 percent of $24 is $1.20; but I already have the $0.90 in my pocket from selling the puts so I can add this to the buck twenty of acceptable loss: $1.20 + $0.90 = $2.10. So if the stock price drops from $25 to $22.90 ($25 - $2.10), I am down 5 percent if I "get put" the stock at $24.

Lots of numbers, I know, but that is how this works. So if Intel drops to $22.90, I need to buy back the puts to be sure that my loss is only 5 percent. I could accept the risk of buying a $1 stock for $23, but that is not the discipline. I don't know what would cause Intel to drop this precipitously, but I didn't think BP could drop from $58 to $29 either. The smart move is to take the loss and buy back the puts. At this point I would need to reevaluate my desire to own Intel and my target buy price.

However, that is only half of the loss-control picture. The other half is minimizing my losses if the stock drops too far or too fast and the put price grows too large. We have set a $1.20 maximum loss for this trade and the puts have the potential to cost more than $23. As the stock price goes down, the puts increase in price. Remember, the only way to avoid buying a $1 stock for $23.10 is to buy back the puts before they grow too expensive. I need to decide ahead of time how high the price of the puts can go before I buy them back.

In our example trade we got $0.90 for the puts when we sold them and we have set our maximum acceptable loss at 5 percent of the contract strike price of $24 ($1.20), so for us to only lose $1.20 on buying back the puts the price of the puts can't go above $2.10 ($2.10 - $0.90 = $1.20).

So, before we enter the trade we must decide that if the puts go to $2.10 we will buy them back—preferably by placing a limit buy order that will be executed only if the put *ask price* reaches this level. You will see how Hannibal could have defeated Rome with this strategy in chapter 3. Note that if we buy back the puts at $2.10, our loss will be $1.20 with nothing to show for it. This is a 100 percent loss of the $1.20.

The Upside
Above was the dark side of selling puts to get an increased—and safe—yield on our money. I picked Intel deliberately because I believe that the

chances that it will drop fast and hard are very low. So, now let's look at the brighter side of the trade. There are several nice eventualities, including:

- The stock stays above $24 during the time we wait for *expiration* of the put contracts. The contracts expire worthless, and we just made $0.90 or 3.6 percent based on the current stock price—more than the dividend we would have earned had we owned the stock for an entire year. We pocket pure profit based on the options deal. At this point we may choose to sell another set of puts to earn more time premium—still ready to buy the stock we want.

- The stock drops just below $24 by expiration and we buy our desired stock at $23.10 instead of $25 for a 7.6 percent savings. The stock does what it has been doing since the market bottom in March 2009—keeps going up gradually—and we earn the 3.6 percent dividend as we watch our principal increase.

These two bullets show the most probable outcomes of selling the puts, but I had to show the dark side first. We need to know the risks of a loss before we can let ourselves be enthralled by the potential profits.

There is much more on risk in chapter 4.

The Next Step

Eventually a put contract we sold is exercised and we are compelled to buy the Intel stock at the contractual price, we get *put* the shares, but at a much lower price than where we first wanted to buy it. We have pocketed the time premium at least once, maybe multiple times, before we get *assigned* the shares. Each time we sold the puts we earned the time premium, which reduced our cost to buy the stock, and since we own it we are earning the dividend. But now we do something else, something that will increase our yield and protect our principal. We *write* a call contract against our stock position—that is, we sell the *covered calls*.

When we sell calls, we are selling a contract that obligates us to sell the contract buyer the underlying stock at the *contract strike price* on the specified *expiration date*. If you sell the calls without owning the stock the call contracts will obligate you to provide, you are "naked" to the downside risk, which is infinite since there is no limit to how high a stock can go. Selling naked calls is more risky then selling naked puts—stocks can't go below zero, but they can go up forever. However, if you own the stock before you write the calls, your losses are covered; hence the name—covered calls.

> **Lesson:** *If you have made profit on a stock and you don't want to sell it, but you do want to protect the profits, you can sell some call options against it. This is called selling covered calls. Your downside protection will be equal to the price of the call you sell or, in market lingo, "write."*

Let's assume we had already completed the put process I described above by the time I looked up the Intel call option prices in mid-July 2012: The October 24 call was selling at $1.90. We could sell the calls and pocket the $1.90 premium. We have purchased our Intel common stock at $23 or lower, depending on how many times we collected the put time premium, so if we need to provide the stock at expiration we are already ahead one dollar—the strike price less our cost ($24 - $23 = $1). But we have also collected the price of the calls we sold, the $1.90 premium, so our new cost basis for the Intel stock we own is $21.10 ($23 - $1.90 = $21.10). Remember we initially wanted to buy Intel at $25. We are already $3.90 (15.6 percent) ahead of our original target price to buy the stock.

Now we are long the Intel common stock and short the October 24 call option. There are only a few well-defined outcomes possible:

- The stock closes above $24 upon option expiration—we are contractually required to sell the stock at $24. But we have collected the quarterly dividend, depending on the stock ex-dividend date, and the call money ($0.21 + $1.90 = $2.11), for an actual profit of 9.2 percent (2.11 ÷ 23 = 9.2 percent)—based on our buy point—in a single quarter, which is an astounding 36.6 percent annual return on our investment. And the process starts all over again.

- The stock moves above $24 *before* expiration—it looks as if we will lose our stock, as explained in the first bullet. But sometimes we find that the call options we are short have not increased in price. We may choose to buy the calls back to maintain ownership of the common stock. This may make sense if the expiration date is very close and the stock is only slightly above the strike price. The portion of the call price that is time premium is very small and, in some cases, if the calls were very spicy when sold, the trading price pumped up by excitement and greed, the call price near expiration can be lower than when we sold them, even if they are *in the money*—that is, the stock price is above the call strike price.

- The stock closes below $24 upon option expiration—the call contract expires worthless, we pocket the premium ($1.90) and keep our Intel common stock with a profit of 8.3 percent based on our buy point (1.90 ÷ 23 = 8.3 percent). Our cost basis for the stock we originally wanted to buy at $25 a share is now $21.10, and we are once again contractually unencumbered and ready to sell another set of calls against our stock position. In this case, we start losing money if the stock drops below $21.10 and we must take action to prevent this—sell the stock, sell a call, or buy a put.

- The stock moves below $24 before expiration—the price of the calls we are short has dropped much more than the price of the stock. We may choose to buy the calls back at a profit before expiration. This may make sense if the expiration date is far away and the stock is only slightly below the strike price—the portion of the call price that is *intrinsic* has disappeared because the stock price is below the strike price. The time premium may also have decreased if the calls were very spicy when sold. New protection can then be added by selling a new set of calls at a lower strike and with a higher premium.

I said above that selling calls against a stock position also protects our principal. The initial buy price of $23 is reduced by the call option premium collected when the covered calls are sold, so the stock price can go down to $21.10 before we start to lose money. If we want more insurance we can buy some naked puts at the time we sell the calls—say, with a $21 strike—and we will be protected below the level of our cost for a very small amount. These puts were at $0.25 when I looked up the call price. The puts will work down to a stock price of zero or until they expire. The combination of selling covered calls and buying puts is called a "collar"—theoretically there is no way to lose money on this structure. But you can still lose if you buy and sell emotionally.

These yields from covered calls and collars are real and so well known that this process is how Bernie Madoff convinced his very sophisticated investors he was making huge profits year in and year out. Unfortunately, Mr. Madoff never placed the trades, he just "made off" with the money.

There is much, much more on option structures and strategies in chapter 5.

On Brokers and Brokerage Houses
I began my investing career in 1978, a year or so after graduating into another jobless recession, similar to the one the kids are facing today. With my degree in biochemistry in hand, I began a fruitless job search as another severe oil-related downturn ravaged the economy. In those days a degree in biochemistry was good only to get into graduate school: medical, pharmacy, or research. I was burned out on school and couldn't do another quarter; I told my mom that if I took one more class I might be the guy diving down the dorm stairwell.

I had been working as a postgraduate research chemist at the University of California–Riverside, when the subtle ultimatum came: enter a doctoral program or get another job. I did manage to get my research published in the *Journal of the American Chemical Society*, though I had to flip hamburgers at night to pay for the last few months of writing. The title of the paper is "Oxidation–Reduction Chemistry of D, L-α-Lipoic Acid, Propanedithiol, and Trimethylene Disulfide in Aprotic and in Aqueous Media." (Really.)

I became a substitute high school teacher in the daytime and a bartender at night. I was working in a disco when the fun 1977 dance movie *Saturday Night Fever* became a huge hit. Starring John Travolta as Tony Manero, the movie that defined the era was directed by John Badham and featured the music of the Bee Gees, the band responsible for much of the iconic music of the late 1970s. Disco nights were everything you might expect from the movie, on a smaller, less-glamorous scale, of course. I was managing a small club in the desert when an old college buddy contacted me about investing in the stock market.

My college buddy had fulfilled his dream of being a professional football player during a short career that was exciting for him but was otherwise unremarkable. It did land him a good job as a stockbroker when it ended. The brokerage firm that hired him believed the competitive nature of sports was a good psychological tell on the mind-set of a future salesman; success in sports foretold success in high-pressure sales. The contacts he had made during his time as a player also fattened his cold call list with highly paid athletes.

In 1977 he had all his clients buying—I remember it well, it was my first trade ever—American Hoist at $19 a share. He was sure that American Hoist was going to be acquired by some bigger fish, so his favorite saying was, "Anytime you have an extra nineteen dollars, buy another share." Well the take-over never happened, and we all lost our shirts. I eventually lost my entire $500 investment. That was my first experience with a stockbroker, and he was one of my closest friends.

It was out of his hands, really. Stockbrokers are salesmen who are required by their companies to push whatever the company is peddling at the time. I was told recently by an ex-broker, who ended up in real estate just in time for the 2006 bust, that we on the outside can never understand the pressure exerted on the brokers to push the products recommended by their companies.

The American Hoist trade was the beginning of a cheap education in the stock market and in trading. Over the following decade I invested what started out as a few hundred dollars at a time but grew to a few thousand, sometimes winning and sometimes losing. But I realized at the time that I was learning the hard lessons of investing with very small trades, preparing for the time when, hopefully, I was much wealthier and would be investing with much larger amounts.

By 1982 I was again working as a chemist, doing applied research for the Electric Power Research Institute. The economy was still in recession, and inflation was still very high. In 1979 the inflation rate reached 13.3 percent, and by 1982 the effective federal funds rates had been raised by Paul Volcker, then the head of the Federal Reserve, to the astounding levels of 21–22 percent. It was this year that the government expanded the individual retirement account. I loved this idea. I took my interest-deductible credit union loan money and opened my first tax-deferred IRA with the $2,000. It just seemed logical. One night some time later, I took a cold call from another young stockbroker. By this time my small nest egg was several thousand dollars in the black—a double on highly speculative stocks.

> **Lesson:** *If you are lucky enough to get a double, you* must *sell half.*

The young broker was very insistent that I get out of stocks and roll into US Treasuries. All I had to do was move my account and buy the Treasury bond fund he was touting. He was very convincing, and I did it. He was, of course, exactly correct and I made a huge return on the investment as interest rates came down and the price of bonds went up. I wish I had never sold the position. In the late 1990s a stockbroker I was working with then told me that he had a client who still owned US Treasuries that were paying 16 percent and had increased in value many times over the years. That was my first positive experience working with a stockbroker—one of the few good ones.

About that time I bought a book called *The Roaring Eighties on Wall Street* by Ira U. Cobleigh and Bruce K. Dorfman. The authors recommended that you apply for as many credit cards as you could get, because the coming bull market would be so big and so long that you should borrow money on the cards to invest in stocks. They were a little over the top and a little early, but they called the bull market, in print, perfectly. I decided going long was a good idea, but borrowing on my credit cards to do it was probably not. The Dow Jones Industrial Average was starting to come back after decades of languishing; I heard the news that it had actually broken 800 when I was listening to AM radio at the laboratory where I worked. That was how I received real-time stock market news back then.

By 1985 I had transitioned from research to sales, taking a job as a sales engineer for a now extinct specialty chemicals company. It was more interesting and much more lucrative, although there were challenges. At one point I had to ask for a major account reassignment because of the then typical two-martini lunch. It was common then to take your customers out to lunch on every visit, and I had customers five days a week who liked to drink. Even though I had ample experience after four years as a bartender, the drinking was too much. After the hard drinking at lunch, the customers would go back to their offices to sleep and I would have to go out into a very dangerous industrial plant to work. I told my boss that I could handle two, maybe three days of liquid lunches a week, but not five. To his credit, he rearranged the accounts so I could have a couple of days off from drinking every week.

During my time working as a sales engineer, in the summer of 1986, news came out that Burroughs was going to buy Sperry and the combined company was to be named Unisys. I saw this as an investment opportunity, and I came into the sales office excited and confident. But when I tried to explain the trade I was taking on, the other engineers in the office thought I was crazy. They couldn't believe I was using options to play a take-over. No amount of explanation could diminish their fear of the unknown. My Burroughs-Sperry trade; my first corporate take-over arbitrage was as foreign to their conservative investment mind-sets as it could be. My idea was to buy the Sperry calls and the Burroughs puts. I hadn't the experience, or the stomach, to sell puts or calls yet. The guys at the office were stunned. They equated stock options with pork bellies and said so. The trade turned out to be quite profitable, but it was my trade, not theirs. They refused to consider how options can make the trade, providing profits with limited risk. They refused to open their minds to the new financial tools.

The 1987 Crash

In the 1980s, you couldn't invest without a stockbroker. It was still a long time before the computer revolution would bring us the investment freedom we enjoy today. You could then, as now, buy a copy of Monday's *Barron's* magazine on Saturday morning at the newsstand. I would spend every weekend reading *Barron's* and studying up for Monday's open. By six o'clock West Coast time on Monday morning I would be waiting in front of my broker's office with checkbook in hand, ready to trade options. It seems incredible now that I actually made money trading options in this painfully slow way. I mostly traded IBM calls, and I remember that IBM was trading then at about $150 a share. In July 2012, after twenty-five years, it was at $200 a share, up from a low of about $90 on March 16, 2009. I also traded the news.

If *Barron's* had a positive news story on a company, I noticed, the stock of that company would pop for a day or two before sinking back down. I would buy the put when the pop happened and sell it back when the happy news died down. I knew when to sell by checking the option quotes in my local newspaper at night after work. I was successful enough that my stockbroker commented, "You must have a friend who works for a newspaper. You seem to know what is going to happen before it does." He obviously wasn't getting up early on Sundays to read *Barron's*.

> **Lesson:** *When a stock moves up suddenly on news, the temptation is to buy call options to take part in the move, but the smart play is to buy put options; the stock will usually pull back near to where it traded before the news was released.*

Then in October 1987 I read a *Barron's* article that informed the world that Merck had developed a new heart medication. That was my signal. When Merck popped on the news, to something like $190 a share, I showed up at the front door of the broker's office with the idea of buying Merck puts. I was ready to plunk down $1,000 for some puts with very little time left to expiration. I sat across from his empty desk for half an hour, drinking coffee from a Styrofoam cup, worried I would be late for work. When my broker finally showed up, I tried to place my order. He had just gotten back from a long European vacation and was not in tune with the markets. When I told him I wanted to buy some Merck puts, he basically called me an idiot.

I remember the conversation well; it was soon to be seared into my memory forever. If this isn't exactly what he said, it is very, very close: "You want to buy puts on Merck, one of the best companies in the world? I'm not our drug company expert, but for you to make anything off them, the entire market would need to crash. I recommend you buy some more of the IBM calls you have been playing."

Swear to God. And that is what I did; I bought the IBM calls. He was able to talk me out of my initial plan and sold me the IBM calls. Within a week, the market did crash; known as Black Monday, the Dow Jones

Industrial Average dropped 503 points on October 19, 1987. This col-lapse still holds the record for the largest single-day percentage loss in the Dow—almost 23 percent. The IBM calls were immediately worthless. I lost everything on the IBM calls I owned and the Merck puts I had wanted to buy increased fortyfold once trading resumed. Merck didn't open again for trading for a week and when it did it was down forty or fifty points. The puts I had wanted to buy would have been worth over $50,000 had I gone through with my initial plan. At that stage in my life and my invest-ment career, that amount of money was gigantic. I never spoke to that broker again; at first I was tempted to go in and call him out for his error, but once I regained rationality I accepted the error was mine.

People are people anywhere in the world, and they will usually act in their own self-interest. I will ignore for now what the bankers did to themselves and the global economy in the lead-up to the 2008 crash. They even surprised one of the biggest free-market cheerleaders, Alan Greenspan, who testified before Congress that the Milton Friedman model of rational markets had not acted rationally. But usually, people will be smart enough to do what is right for themselves. The trick is to find out what *they* think is good for them.

During the 1990s, while I was negotiating engineering contracts for new chemical and power infrastructure in the People's Republic of China, I quickly learned that the only way to be sure of a deal was to understand what the Chinese negotiator wanted—for himself, not for his company. In those days, and to some degree even now, the saying was, "A signed contract in China is only the beginning of the negotia-tions." So it was important that my goals were aligned with the goals of the Chinese negotiator sitting across from me. On one huge deal in Shanxi Province (pronounced shan-she), the Chinese guy was control-ling a $2 billion construction project, but his primary interest was how much warm beer he could sell to the construction workers in the karaoke bar that he had purchased just before construction began.

That is why I say, "Listen to investment advisors, but never blindly follow their advice." Their motivations are not your motivations; their goals are not aligned with your goals. Most stockbrokers do not make money from investing, they make their money from the commissions they get from your trades—win or lose.

> **Lesson:** *A stockbroker is a great guy, but he is a salesman, not an investment expert. You can't depend on him for investment advice. You are on your own.*

I have always regretted missing being short Merck when the 1987 crash hit. For many years after the crash I would fantasize about having a framed copy of the front page of the newspaper hanging on the wall my office for all to see, its three-inch headline screaming, "Dow Down 503," my buy and sell slips for the puts mounted on either side of the story. I wanted to have it on the wall to show that I had made money when everyone else had lost money. I ran into the broker at a golf course a few years later and he didn't even recognize me; so much for stockbrokers. That was the last time I actually traded on anything a stockbroker said. I listen, but I make up my own mind.

I still have the newspaper stored somewhere, but now I do have some even more successful trading slips hanging on my walls. The Merck put deal didn't happen, but it was burned into my trading consciousness, never very far from the surface for the next twenty years. More important, as the years went by, I came to realize that the best part of the crash wasn't the shorting opportunity just before the crash, it was the huge buying opportunity that came immediately afterward. I became a predator—even better, a flea—stalking the big dogs, waiting for the next opportunity. It came in 2007.

By late 2007, I had been investing and learning from my mistakes for so long that I'd gotten pretty good at it. I finally had to give up my day job to concentrate on my investments full time. Trading stops being a hobby when your investments bring home more than your day job for a few years and the IRS tells you they want quarterly tax payments. Lots of taxes are a good thing; they indicate that you are making lots of money. That said, no one wants to pay more than their fair share, and it is a simple thing to avoid paying more than you should—all you need to do is plan your strategy and execute your plan. A good accountant can help with the plan, and there are also many great books you can choose to read—some are listed in the bibliography at the end of this book. *The Roaring Eighties on Wall Street* is there too, but I still don't recommend buying stocks with a credit card.

Venture Capital

If you have accumulated some wealth, you will invariably be contacted by someone you trust who will offer you a position on the "ground floor" of a company that will soon be the next Apple, Microsoft, or whatever. This happened to me several times and each time the deals turned out poorly. I offer the embarrassing story below as a word of warning. I finally got my money back out of this venture capital deal not by the fantastic technology of the start-up or by the thoughtful guidance of its management but by trading the virtually worthless paper on the over-the-counter market for almost five years. Other venture investors, who didn't have the time to do this kind of trading, are still way underwater. My advice to anyone thinking of putting his or her money to work in a venture capital investment is to keep it personal. You may want to consider the investment if you think you can add something to the success of the start-up, other than just money; but invest only if you plan to be an active member of the company and can provide tangible assistance to the company's chances for success.

Enable IPC (EIPC)

Enable IPC has patented a process that creates a microscopic die used in a nanosize foundry to create a surface studded with tiny rod-shaped projections. In my imagination it looks like the guy's face and whiskers in the shaving lotion commercials—millions, no billions, of tiny rods sticking out of the surface. The benefit of the process is an exponential increase in the material's surface area. This is especially important in capacitors and batteries, and this is the business Enable has chosen. Enable's capacitors kick the butts of everything else out there.

I first became involved with Enable Intellectual Property Commercialization (Enable IPC, Enable, or EIPC—the stock market trade symbol) before the crash of 2008. Enable had approached my investment company, Cheyenne Capital Corporation, with a request for venture-capital financing.

In the original deal, Cheyenne lent Enable venture capital under terms very favorable to Cheyenne. The loan was of short duration, with a high interest rate, and Enable was also required to award Cheyenne a large number of warrants. Similar to a call option, a warrant gives the owner the right to buy common stock at a set—usually low—price at or before some later date. One important difference is that a warrant usually has time measured in years while an option usually expires in months.

After the economy had tipped over, money had become very scarce for start-up companies like EIPC, and EIPC fell further and further behind in the repayment to Cheyenne of its venture loan. I finally agreed to convert the outstanding debt to EIPC stock. At the height of the crash, in 2008, when the lack of capital threatened to crush Enable, Cheyenne agreed to invest another tranche that was almost as large as the first. This tranche also came with stock warrants. After this investment Cheyenne needed to file a form 13G with the Securities and Exchange Commission to announce we had acquired more than a 10 percent ownership share in a publicly traded company.

How, I wondered, did I ever get to this point?

The first tranche stock price was $0.025 per share after interest earned on the original loan was subtracted and the stock price of the second tranche was $0.030 per share. By the end of 2008, Cheyenne had millions of shares.

In early 2010, I began to believe that the investment had been a poor one, driven by ego and the same thought processes that lead people to buy lottery tickets every week. In my capacity of chief investment officer for Cheyenne, I began to monetize losses on the outstanding shares and sold over half the position at about $0.015 per share. By late 2010 the share value of EIPC had dropped to less than $0.0035 per share. In December 2010 the shares had reached such a low level—I had watched them bounce off that level several times—that I began to buy back the position, more than tripling the number of shares Cheyenne owned by the end of April 2011. The average basis price of the "new" shares was $0.0045 per share.

Then Enable's luck finally changed. Its new nanocapacitor and solar powered radio frequency identification (RFID) tag was featured in a nanotechnology journal. *At last a little recognition!* And the RFID tag, designed to be stapled to the ears of cattle, seemed to have a ready and eager customer base. I was keeping my fingers crossed, but Enable looked as if it might start generating some positive cash flow sometime soon. The news getting out, even if only to the narrow world of nanonerds, generated a huge amount of buying pressure in EIPC. As the stock price approached $0.015 again, with the "new" shares up over 300 percent, Cheyenne began to sell into the demand. Cheyenne needed to sell some of what had become a very large position in Enable as part of a routine portfolio balancing. Whenever a position doubles, it is my policy to sell at least half of the position.

Jesse Livermore, the infamous trader who was gloriously *short* the market in October 1929, said, "When you are selling out, it is no wiser or braver to sell fifty shares than fifty thousand shares; but fifty shares you can sell in the dullest market without breaking the price, and fifty thousand shares of a single stock is a different proposition." Cheyenne Capital had so many shares of Enable to sell that only a very robust market could absorb the selling pressure Cheyenne would produce without the price breaking down. Livermore also said that if a lucky circumstance helps you to get out, you take advantage of that circumstance. His "lucky" circumstance to close out a huge short position was the sinking of the *Lusitania* in 1915.

The market in EIPC had been nonexistent for three years, but the trade article brought it back healthy and strong, if only temporarily. The surge in trading volume provided the first opportunity for Cheyenne to sell the large number of EIPC shares we needed to sell. During a two-week period, Cheyenne was the primary seller of EIPC shares, as much as 75 percent of the daily volume. When Cheyenne's selling was finished, the overall investment in EIPC looked like it would be profitable—up double digits at the time, if interest and consulting fees were included and if the many warrants held could be exercised and the resulting stock monetized; two years later that doesn't seem too likely. The remaining shares and warrants provide almost all the profit from the original venture capital investment; if the stock drops to zero, and the warrants expire worthless, which seems very likely, the relationship will be a painful, if small loser of about 2 percent.

Five years of work and worry to lose 2 percent is not my kind of deal and tracking the buying and selling of millions of shares caused a tax accounting nightmare that cost more in accounting fees than I lost on the entire deal. The worst part of it is that all the trading needed to get back to even distracted me from other, potentially more profitable trades of more established companies.

Chapter 2

Bulls and Bears

I'm Comfortable Being a Flea

What would a book like this be without a quote from Oliver Stone's 1987 classic movie, *Wall Street*? This stock market movie starred Michael Douglas as the greedy Gordon Gekko, Charlie Sheen as Bud Fox, the kid stockbroker who will do anything to get to the top, and the spectacularly beautiful Daryl Hannah as the money-conscious blond bombshell, with a very special bonus of Martin Sheen, Charlie's real-life father, as Bud's union leader dad.

What investor can ever forget the speech Douglas's character, Gekko, makes at the annual meeting to the shareholders of Teldar Paper, a company he plans to destroy for his personal profit? The speech has become an iconic example of the greed of the 1980s and of corporate raiders in general:

"America has become a second-rate power. Its trade deficit and its fiscal deficit are at nightmare proportions...The new law of evolution in corporate America seems to be survival of the un-fittest. Well, in my book you either do it right or you get eliminated...I am not a destroyer of companies; I am a liberator of them! The point is, ladies and gentlemen, that greed—for a lack of a better word—is good. Greed is right. Greed works. Greed clarifies, cuts through, and captures the essence of the evolutionary spirit. Greed, in all its forms—greed for life, for money, for love, knowledge—has marked the upward surge of mankind. And greed—you mark my words—will not only save Teldar Paper, but that other malfunctioning corporation called the USA."

Wow! Who can argue with that logic?

***

Traders and investors often speak of the Dow Jones Industrial Average, but we rarely remember one of the pioneers of stock market investing, Charles Dow. He was one of the first traders to use stock charting as an analysis tool. He started the Wall Street Journal and was the first analyst to create a stock market index. His theories about the way the markets work are still used by traders today. One of my favorite Dow quotes is, "The man who begins to speculate in stocks with the intention of making a fortune usually goes broke, whereas the man who trades with a view of getting good interest on his money sometimes gets rich."

On one of the six screens of my trading computer I have some Post-it Notes. On these slips of sticky paper I have written two short warnings for me to notice while in the chaos of the trading day. They are rules an options trader must live by:

- Don't be slow.

- Don't be greedy.

Greed may have worked for the robber barons and sharks Gekko listed in his speech, and for him. But for a trader, Greed is an enemy that steals profits and expands losses. There is an old Wall Street saying: "Bulls get rich, bears get rich, but pigs get slaughtered."

The theme of this book is:

In the stock market there are bulls and there are bears. One or the other is always in the lead. I just want to be a flea—small enough not to get noticed and nimble enough to hop from one to the other for a tiny bite.

I believe everyone, whether or not they trade, is inherently either:

- a stock market bull; or

- a stock market bear.

Before you can be a stock market flea, you need to know if your natural tendency is to be a bull or to be a bear. My inherent tendency is to be a stock market bull. I make more money in a bull market than in a bear market. I have a buddy who is inherently a bear and says he does much better shorting stocks when they go down than buying them when they go up. The important thing is to know what your natural tendencies are. A bull will tend to buy too soon and tend to hold on too long, while a bear will tend not to buy early enough and tend not to hold stock long enough. It is an optimism versus pessimism thing, I think—the glass half full or half empty. I once thought that I could simply change from a bull to a bear and make the same money both ways—to be a true flea. I have since learned that it is not so easy to go against my inherent tendency to optimism. Jesse Livermore put it this way: "A trader...must also know himself and provide against his own weaknesses."

On January 28, 2009, I put on a trade that exemplifies what I mean by trying to trade like a bear when I am a natural bull. To stretch the animal metaphor—a tiger can't change its stripes. Below is the entry I made in my trading log in its entirety.

28 Jan 09

Today I took off the short position in Treasuries I have been holding for over a month. The Fed announced today that they would support low interest rates by purchasing Treasuries. Great. You can't fight the Fed. I was waiting for a 10 percent gain. It made it up to about plus 6 percent at one point, but I only got out with a 3.8 percent gain. Once out of the Treasury trade, I reinvested the proceeds in put options on AutoZone (AZO). Put options are a bet the stock price will decrease.

The logic for thinking AutoZone will go up is compelling. Since no one is buying new cars, people will need to take care of their old, high-maintenance cars for a while longer and will need to buy stuff from AutoZone. Fine, but this assumes people can, and will, do a little of their own car maintenance: oil changes, rubber hose and fan belt replacements, bulb replacements, and maybe, just maybe, something as complicated as a battery replacement. The kind of stuff we did as teenagers. OK, for the sake of argument, I'll agree to all that. Everyone is going to go to AutoZone to buy their light maintenance items. I'll even ignore the fact that oil has dropped 70 percent because of the precipitous decline in demand for gasoline, indicating that people are driving much less.

The thing is, the last time I went into an AutoZone to buy a twenty-dollar part, not that long ago, I bought some car wax and some lint-free towels to go with it, and some spray for the windows, and some cool reversible-ratchet box wrenches... Oh, and the key chain at the check-out counter. My twenty-dollar part was now about $100 at check-out. The increase in my receipt was due to the eighty dollars of retail items I had added to my cart.

Retail? Retail? Retail has been obliterated over the last year, but not AutoZone. Today AutoZone closed at $137.27 per share. This is the same price level it had in August 2008. Every other stock in the world has taken a big hit since then. Even Walmart got hammered over that period. The old-timers on the Street say that in a bear market, no stock is safe; every stock will take a hit eventually as the market reaches a new, lower equilibrium. The stock price of AutoZone seems to be artificially out of equilibrium with the rest of the market and way out of step with the other retail stocks. If 80 percent of AutoZone revenues is due to spontaneous purchases of retail items, it doesn't add up.

But let me go back to the "everybody under the car" premise. I don't buy it; it is just as likely, I believe, that most people will drive less and extend the time they wait before performing routine maintenance.

AutoZone reports earnings on March 10 or thereabouts. One data service indicated this morning that the earnings estimate was about $1.80 a share. If they miss this estimate in this market, they'll be eviscerated. They also say that there was 8.8 percent short interest in the stock and that this was up 25 percent recently, but a lot of these shorts may have been forced out today with the gain of more than $3 in the stock price. The options expire on March 21, so there will be time between earnings and expiration.

The Mar 125 put (AZOOE) closed at $5.50 today, the Mar 120 put (AZOOD) closed at $4.20. I bought the Mar 120 put. Now I have seven weeks for the stock to drop the way I think it will. If I am wrong, I will probably be forced out of the position to limit losses at about $3.50, but if I am right, the Mar 120 put could increase to about $9 with the stock at about $125 per share and continue to increase dollar for dollar as the stock drops below $120 per share. The overall market is down about 40 percent, and retail stocks are down as much as 70 percent. If AutoZone were to drop by 15 percent from here, it would retest its October 08 low of about $107 and the Mar 125 put could trade for more than $20. If AutoZone retests its November 08 low of about $92, the put could trade for over $30.

30 Jan 09

AutoZone is down $2.56 to 134.71 or 1.9 percent. The Mar120 put trade is up $0.80 or 19 percent. I am going to keep these over the weekend because I think AZO has more room on the downside.

I should have taken the money and run. AutoZone never broke; its share price continued to climb for years and my so well-thought-out put strategy expired worthless. On March 23, 2011, the share price was $266 and by July 2012 it was an incredible $365. The worst part of this trade was I didn't follow my plan to stop loss by selling at $3.50. This is what I mean when I say I do better as a bull; this was me trying to be a bear.
Not my personality.

On Thursday, October 13, 2011, I sent out this mea culpa in my market letter: "Here is one I got very wrong. AutoZone is trading at $326.62 right now. Up 138 percent since I bad-mouthed it on Jan

28, 2009, just before the market bottom in March. The puts expired worthless."

I quickly received this response from one of my readers: "Your initial puts may have been worthless, but were you prescient early enough to recognize your analytical error and go long?" My response to the reader was a little embarrassing, but there was a lesson in the bad AutoZone trade.

"Nope. Once you get an idea it is hard to force yourself to continue to look at the facts. (A current problem in politics, I think. You should be party to the e-mail discussion about Keynesian economics I'm having right this minute. Only I am so outnumbered I can't add another smart adversary to the argument.) I let the options expire, but I had a very nice profit in the first week or so after buying them. The options discipline told me to sell some and take profit, but I was too greedy. I therefore broke the second of my own *two cardinal rules* of options trading:

1. Don't be slow.

2. Don't be greedy.

Had I not taken such a public opinion on the stuff, I might have done better. This has happened to me more than once. The market runs on emotion and ego, fear and greed. As Dirty Harry said, "A man's got to know his limitations."

Lesson: *A public pronouncement cements you into a position.*

Once you understand who you are and what your tendencies will lead you to do—compel you to do—you can watch out for them and use a predetermined plan to trade or buy insurance (options) to protect yourself from them. It is important to remember that no trade stands alone. The trades you made last week, month, or year will remain in your psyche much longer than in your account. If you lose money on a trade you will be prejudiced to any change for the better; your pain will keep you out of the new trade. Also, your losers affect your attention and your psyche—sell them. Winners, on the other hand, tend to increase the risk you are willing to take; be aware that big wins can cause you to throw caution to the wind in subsequent trades.

> **Lesson:** *Past trades will affect future trading. A big loss could cause you to miss a great opportunity, while a big win could deaden your appreciation of risk.*

Everything in your life affects your trading: your emotional state, the feelings of those around you, your last winning trades and losers, conversations with other traders, things said on television and in newspapers, whether you are sick or well, happy or sad, angry, lonely, or drunk. Everything adds its weight, heavy or light, to the burden of decision making. Everything in your perception makes its contribution to your trading success or failure.

I have a good friend who became a successful financial planner and money manager, and a very good trader. We played high school football together, him quite well and me not so much. When other old friends from the team ask why he is so aloof, so difficult to contact, and so impossible to maintain a friendship with, I just say, "He is a trader." But since they don't trade, it is impossible for them to understand that every interaction has the potential of ruining a trade, and with the amounts of other people's money my friend trades, he can't afford too many ruined trades.

On Monday, September 15, 2008, the markets were hugely down, as I had expected. I wrote in my trading log,

> Lehman Brothers has declared bankruptcy. I expected this to happen last Thursday and then last Friday. I knew that if the Lehman deal didn't get done there would be a huge down day on Monday, today. But I didn't have the guts to hold onto my Research in Motion puts because

they only had five days until expiration. I felt this was going to happen. I even looked at some Goldman Sachs put options last week. The RIMM puts I sold for an $8,000 loss a few days ago would have been made me a $56,000 profit, had I held them until today.

When I made that entry I hadn't yet added up the total missed opportunity from selling too soon. I had closed out another set of RIMM puts on the September 8 with a $13,000 win, but by September 15 they would have been worth over $100,000. And with the markets in full meltdown after the Lehman bankruptcy, both sets of puts doubled again overnight. By the close of trading on Tuesday, September 16, the set I sold on September 8 was worth $208,000 and the set I had written about in my trading log on September 15 were at $126,000. Although the trade was a net winner, the total missed opportunity was well over a third of a million dollars, had I held the first set for another week and the last set for just two more sessions.

But my personal life got in the way. I was scheduled to take a long weekend vacation and didn't want to have a big position when I couldn't trade. I didn't want to worry about the position and the puts were so stale (five days left) you could smell them, so I sold too early. Options are like houseguests and fish; they start to smell after three days.

On Tuesday, September 16, 2008, I wrote,

> Had I held the all RIMM puts I sold last week to today's open I would have made $350,000 on them instead of $5,000…This single trade would have made my year and made me a great deal of money from the crash. IF, IF, IF.

It is impossible to separate your personal life from your trading life. If you are not ready to make some sacrifices in your trading profits *and* in your personal relationships, you should not try to trade.

Chapter 3

Emotion

It's All about You, or You Are Your Own Worst Enemy

In the 2004 movie *King Arthur*, starring Clive Owen as the nascent King Arthur and Keira Knightley as his blue-painted barbarian queen Guinevere, Arthur and his warrior comrades are Roman soldiers stationed at the northernmost posting of Rome in England just as the empire is coming apart at the seams. Winston Churchill, in his book *The Birth of Britain*, credits the Arthurian myth to the last, isolated glimmer of Roman civilization on the island receding into the chaos of the Dark Ages.

When Arthur stands against the hordes of Cedric, the barbarian king, he tells him, "I came to see your face so that I alone may find you on the battlefield. And it will be good of you to mark my face, Saxon, for the next time you see it; it will be the last thing you see on this earth." And as Arthur rides off, Cedric says, "Ah, finally, a man worth killing."

That is the best quote for this book, but my favorite quote from the movie comes when Lancelot warns Guinevere, "There's a large number of lonely men out there." And Guinevere answers, "Don't worry, I won't let them rape you."

***

The most important things a new trader needs to learn are not details about the markets or the mechanics of trading; the most important lessons are about the trader himself or herself. If you feel good, confident, and sure of the trade, you are apt to make the right decisions. I can't say if the trade will make money or not, but the results will be better. If the trader is feeling down, the trades will reflect this in a negative way.

No matter how smart or tough we are, we are all still controlled by our emotions. When Hannibal entered Italy from the north in about 218 BCE, the Romans dispatched a huge army to meet him. Hannibal had 100,000 men and Rome had almost as many, but Hannibal's army was an undisciplined mob of loosely allied enemies of Rome and the Roman army was a highly trained force of professional soldiers—the best in the world. The Roman army's strength was the legion, the shield-to-shield line of battle, but their weakness came when they were not in formation as they traveled. As the Romans marched north along the Po River, the Carthaginians and their allies waited in a thick fog that blanketed the steep hills rising from the river. When Hannibal attacked, the Romans were completely surprised and, unfortunately for them, still in marching formation. The battle was a slaughter; the Romans were annihilated in a way only possible in ancient times, hacked to death one by one without mercy, over a period of hours long after the outcome of the battle had been established.

After an even gorier bloodletting of a second Roman army at the battle of Cannae in 216 BCE, the door to Rome was open. If Hannibal had marched on to Rome immediately after the battle, the war would have

been won. But that is not what he did. Hannibal waited, and in waiting he allowed the Romans to bring in legions from the far-off prov-
inces to man their city walls. That was another strength of Rome—their
empire-wide transportation system. After more than two millennia, no one
can be sure why Hannibal, a veteran of many gruesome battles and a warrior since childhood, could not cope with the butchery he had wrought on
the fields of Cannae, a battle that gave meaning to the word carnage. Some
say he was surprised by the speed and the magnitude of his victory and
had no plan for the follow-up attack; others say he was emotionally damaged at the sight of over a hundred thousand dead men in such a small area.

But let's stretch our imaginations to include some modern-day, electronic stock-trading tools. Suppose Hannibal had placed some electronic
orders with stop-loss sell orders (run away) for the eventuality of a loss and
some electronic buy orders (move on to Rome) to be executed in the event of
a win. These predetermined actions would have occurred regardless of his
emotional state. At the end of the victorious battle the buy orders would have
been activated and his army would have marched on. He would have taken
Rome in months rather than wandering around Italy for ten years, always
outside the city walls, never reaching his goal, eventually losing the war.

There is a theory about how the stock market works that conflicts
with the so-called rational market theory that got us into the current
mess. I will go into the details of the rational market and efficient market
theories in subsequent chapters of this book and in great detail in chapter 10. Here it is sufficient to state that the crash of 2008 has debunked
the concept of naturally self-regulating markets. Juxtaposed to the
fallen rational and efficient market theories is human emotion theory
(HUEMO), which explains how banks like Lehman Brothers and insurance companies like American International Group (AIG) could have
behaved so irrationally leading up to the crash.

HUEMO is a system that includes human psychological factors
in the understanding of how markets work and how human emotion
affects stock prices and causes sea changes in the entire system of markets. I don't believe HUEMO is antithetical to traditional techniques

of stock-price analysis: evaluations of corporate fundamentals and technical analysis of the charts. I think the two go together like peanut butter and jelly—and just about as messily.

Economist Martin Shubik designed a simple game to elucidate how rational people with perfect information can make disastrously irrational decisions. Although there are many variations of the game, the most famous is the twenty-dollar-bill auction. A non-zero sum sequential game, the twenty-dollar-bill auction is a classic psychology experiment that can tell us a lot about the markets. In the game the moderator auctions off a twenty-dollar bill with bidding starting at one dollar and subsequent bids must be in one-dollar increments. Who wouldn't bid a dollar for a twenty? But the rules of the game are that the winner of the bidding pays his last bid, but *the last losing bidder pays what they bid as well.*

In the game I watched, many different players actively bid early in the game, while the bidding was still in single digits. But as the game went on only two bidders were left and as their bids closed in on twenty dollars the reality of the game sank in, but by this time it was too late to get out. After the bids exceed $20, the point of the bidding is to avoid being the loser. In the game I saw, the winner bid $28 and the loser $27, so the winner lost $8 and the loser lost $27. But in many iterations of the game the bidding goes far beyond this because the winner will lose less than the loser by getting the twenty for his winning bid. In one game the winner paid $54 and the loser paid $53—the winner lost $34 and the loser lost $53. The rational thing would be to stop bidding much earlier, but we humans are not really that rational, and neither are our markets. John Maynard Keynes famously said, "The markets can remain irrational longer than you can stay solvent."

Rational market theory of how markets and stock prices are valued depends on the huge assumption that stock traders make decisions in a completely rational and objective manner. It assumes that the traders have and incorporate all public information into their decision-making process. The problem is that in the real world, outside of the ivory tower universities where the theories were created, things don't work so prettily. This has been shown in one empirical study after another. Traders make decisions emotionally, despite using every available tool to control this tendency. The same data can be interpreted in vastly different ways, depending on the emotional state of the trader, making black-and-white hypotheses such as the rational market theory work right up to the point where they don't. Why did AIG traders keep writing credit default swaps on Lehman Brothers, taking on sixty times the liability of Lehman, even though the consequences of that action could have destroyed the banking system? The mental state of a trader not only affects his view of the market and his expectations, but it can actually affect the cognitive performance of his mind.

The influence of emotional trading can be easily seen in the pricing of stocks that do not always reflect the value of the underlying company. Prices are routinely moved up and down by the mood of the markets. Prices go up unreasonably during bull markets and down just as unreasonably during bear markets. This phenomenon is what gives rise to the expansion of bubbles in the market. I will spare you another rendition of the Dutch tulip bulb mania of 1637, but that bubble was the same as the dot-com bubble of 2001 and the real estate bubbles of 2008 *and* 1929.

Emotional trading is happening right now, as millions of people saving for their retirement are terrified to come back into the stock market because they still sting from the losses they incurred in 2008, even though the valuations of stocks and the stock market are at historic lows. In March 2009, when a friend asked me what stocks I was buying, I told him, "Right now it doesn't matter. You could tape the stock tables from a newspaper on the wall and throw darts at it and in a few years everyone would think you were a genius." I was buying Freeport McMoran at $10 (split adjusted) and Apple at $132—genius, but I also sold them for what I thought at the time were "huge" profits. Both are now fivefold where I sold them.

Traders are always trying to figure out the emotional state of the markets, ready to pounce if they think there is a direction to the emotion—up or down. That is why they, and I, listen to the TV mavens, and newspaper gurus, and even the crazy bloggers. The problem is, when everyone gets the same idea, markets can tank for no reason, leaving the traditional guys—the valuation and technical guys—shaking their heads in confusion.

To protect ourselves from our own emotions, we need to plan ahead and execute that plan emotionlessly. Say you love to play blackjack so you go to Las Vegas. The first thing you do when you get there is to visit the blackjack tables to gamble. Let's say you win your first few hands. Your emotions—your gambling (trading) emotions—soar, and maybe because you have been winning and your emotions are out of control, you let everything ride. All of your emotions will be elevated: your fear will go up because you have more to lose than you did initially, and your greed will go up because now you have so much more to gain. Whichever side of your ego wins will motivate your decision to let it all ride again or take the money and walk away. These emotions need to be controlled with rules made *before* the emotions kick in. The only way to control these human emotions is by having a well-thought-out plan and executing that plan. In Vegas it helps to have a considerate spouse yank you out of the pits by the ear.

To stretch the gambling analogy a little bit (but in options trading not that far), you need to take some of your winnings and put them in your pocket. Don't let the rows of pretty chips mesmerize you. In the options market you need to control your natural greed and sell into a winning position. The worst thing gamblers do, and they do it all the time, is to double the size of their bet when they lose. What kind of a system is that? Yes, you might win the next hand and get back to even, but if the cards you are dealt are dogs, you just took a big loss and tripled it!

Dennis Gartman is on TV all the time. He is a famous and successful commodities trader and has a newsletter in wide circulation. Every year, on the last day before the holiday break in December, he goes on TV and recites his rules of trading. Here is Dennis Gartman's Number One Rule of trading:

"Never average into a losing position. It's good to average up. The market is telling you that you are wrong, or right. Trading is psychological and by averaging into a loser you diminish your mental state and it prevents you from taking on new positions."

John Elway was one of the best football quarterbacks of all time. He said something about trying too hard to win that is perfect for the options market and for blackjack too:

"When it's going wrong, and you are a character guy, you try harder, and sometimes that works against you."

I saw this in myself when I was in sales with Betz Laboratories. Early in my time as a sales manager, one of the smart young engineers who reported to me said, just before he took another job, "You are so intense." Intense? I'm intense? It was news to me. But truer words were never spoken. I *was* intense; much too intense for my own good. But when I came home from my first trip to China in 1992, I was a changed soul. I had seen outside the bubble and had realized that my life was not all I wanted it to be. I decided to work less and to write more; to allow the quantity, if not the quality, of my work to slip and to ignore the company rules and requirements, to run the business as I thought best. If Betz didn't like it, they could fire me. I could not have cared less about my sales numbers or the grind of selling new customers. I went into the plants less often and I took customers golfing more often—I *was* always there when they needed me, but I didn't go in just to fill out a call report. The surprising thing was that my sales numbers went up and I sold several critical new accounts. All I had to do was let go and relax.

A few days before the generational bottom in March 2009, I bought Freeport-McMoran (FCX) at $21 a share, equivalent to $10.50 per share in after-split terms. FCX is the biggest producer of copper in the world. In those hectic, even chaotic, days, I was mostly making ultra-short-term option trades, but I wanted to build a long-term portfolio of great stocks that had been beaten down during the crisis and were paying high dividends. I figured that if the market recovered and the stocks went up, I would get a capital gain and still have the dividend. And if the stock went up more than the yearly dividend yield, I'd cash in and find some other dividend stock to buy. Back then good companies had become suspect; FCX had dropped from $75 to $21 and its dividend had increased to 8 or 9 percent. This was my reason for owning it. A nice dividend has a stabilizing affect on the price of a stock.

The day after I bought FCX, the company announced that they were suspending the dividend. *Crap, I couldn't have timed that much worse.* So now my reason for buying the stock was gone: it no longer had any dividend. It opened the next day at $15—*crap, crap, crap.* Now I was a seller: My reason for buying and continuing to own the stock was gone. It no longer paid a dividend, and in a day, it was down more than 20 percent from my buy point. Since FCX no longer fit the reason I had bought it in the first place, I readied myself to sell and in a couple of days it had bounced up to $25—up more than 20 percent from where I bought it. Up more than twice the amount of the annual dividend I had originally sought when I bought the stock. I had to sell. That was the discipline. My reason for holding the equity was gone and I had doubled the yearly return I had expected to receive from it—I had to sell. And I did.

But...I could have bought the stock back anytime during the next two years and still made money—the move up during that time was so strong and so consistent. FCX continued to move up all through 2010, trading at almost $119 on January 4, 2011. The stock split two to one effective February 1, 2011. I missed most of this move, but I did do well on some naked calls and a call spread in late 2010, catching a little of the upward momentum.

Let me dream: a thousand shares times the difference (119 - 21 = 98) is $98,000 in profit. Yep, should have held on to that one, but then I should have held onto everything I owned in March 2009, the generational bottom, after what may turn out to be the crash of the century.

I can even dream bigger than that. What would have been the result if I had instead become bullish on FCX and bet the farm on it at $15 a share, the day after the dividend was suspended? I could have done quite well investing, say, $1 million at $15 a share. This would have been 66,000 shares. And if I had sold all these shares where it was trading on January 15, 2011, two years later, at $120, I would have bagged $7.9 million. On that one trade, I'd be finished trading forever. The opportunity was there, but I didn't have the courage or the conviction I needed to become a winner. I coached high school football instead; the kids were big winners, going nine and one for the season.

But by July 2012 the floor had come out from under FCX and it was trading at less than $34 a share, still almost three times where I sold it, but no fortune would have been made had I not sold at the peak, as in my daydream. That is the real key to trading, not what or where you buy, but how you manage the sale. Selling FCX by my plan I made good profit and avoided risk. Daydreams are fun, but they are just daydreams. My FCX trade did teach me an important lesson that I used several times during the downdraft: the news of a dividend suspension was almost always good for the price of the equity. It signaled the time to buy.

Selling is the hard part. We can do all our homework and find a great stock or a great option, buy it, achieve our initial goal, and watch our profits dwindle away over time as we fidget, finger on the selling trigger. Knowing when to sell is one thing, overcoming our own psychology to actually sell is another. There are many lessons, and wives' tales, about when to sell, and I have some rules about selling. Here are a few reasons to sell that have been burned into my gray matter:

- If you are ever lucky enough to get a double, sell half. This rule is unimpeachable and never changing.

- Selling is the best part of a trade. I love to sell. It is like leaping into a cool pond on a hot day.

- If you buy a stock or an option, you must have a plan. Work your plan. Sell when you planned. Don't get caught in mission creep. It has been said that in battle, the plan goes out the window with the first shot fired. But they also say that the fog of war makes real-time decisions almost impossible once the battle is joined. I think I would rather follow the plan than to improvise when I can't see what is going on.

- Use trailing stop-loss orders, in percentage terms, for stocks. I like to use a 5 percent trailing stop from the first time the stock turns down after I buy it. In percentage terms the trailing stop will go up with the stock and will grow larger, in dollar terms, as the stock rises. I like to wait for the stock to move up 5 percent before I trust the automation, this will help avoid getting stopped out below my buy price if the stock gets hit with a temporary loss too early. Remember the so-called Flash Crash of May 6, 2010? Many investors who had been smart enough to put on stop orders got taken out by the computer glitch at low levels for huge losses, only to have the stock they had sold recover to near normal levels by the end of the day.

- Don't use trailing stops when trading options. It would be great if you could use these but option volatility forces us to use too large a stop to avoid getting stopped out by the noise. Sometimes you can use a specific price to trigger the sale. Say you bought an option at $3; you might not want to take more than a $1 loss so you put in a stop loss for a bid price of $2 to sell at the asking price, although this won't guarantee you get out. To be more positive, you could sell at the bid price, but if the market is thin, you may still not get out. It is best to watch them closely and sell manually.

- When trading options, think about it like hitting a baseball. You want to make lots of singles and the occasional double. You shouldn't expect to hit home runs. When an option trades up 30–50 percent in a couple of days or less, it is always tempting to sell, and you probably should. A nonsell is just like a buy. If you hold onto the position, you must reevaluate at each new—higher or lower—option value.

- Don't let outside distractions or data influence your decision to sell or not to sell: no artificial goals for the day, the week, the month, and so on; no specific amount of profit desired to make up for a prior loss; no specific amount needed for something you want to buy; no outside, irrelevant information should bias your decision. It's easier said than done.

I always feel happy when I sell. I should sell more. I even felt happy selling the last 1,000 shares of BP at the very bottom of its notorious decline in 2010. I sold the very cheapest shares sold at $29, but I felt happy and relieved when it was done. Anything to relieve the stress; stress is an enemy of smart selling.

It is easy to buy a good stock; you have all the time in the world to do your research and can pick the exact moment to buy. But selling is different; the time to sell comes to you, you do not pick it. Hope is also an enemy of profitable selling. Hope is that moment when you hit your stop-loss point, but you convince yourself that you would only be locking in losses—such as I did with BP—and you hold the loser as it continues to decline.

Yep, you are locking in losses, true enough. But they are usually locked in at a higher point than if you wait. I always try to think of it this way (and trying isn't easy): "I am right, it *is* coming back up; but I can make profit faster using the money to buy something else." This gets you out of the trade without the need to go through the psychological effort of admitting that your original premise was incorrect. Many of the experts say, "The happiness of winning is half the pain of losing." An optimistic trader like me, will use hope to avoid the pain of admitting losses. Here are a couple of other things I try to watch for in my trading:

- The Endowment Effect—we humans always think things are worth more when we own them. We always want more for something we are selling than we would pay for the same thing if we were buying.

- The Status Quo Effect—the human tendency to do nothing. Our preference to maintain a position rather than make a change, bullish or bearish. This is deadly for an options trader, because the clock is always running.

- The Disposition Effect – the way excess risk avoidance can cause us to sell our winners too soon and our losers too late. (This is an ongoing battle for a retired guy like me, with no outside income to compensate for trading mistakes.)

During the US Open, one television announcer said, "After years as a professional golfer I have learned that when you hit into trouble, get out of trouble, minimize your mistake. Don't go from trouble to more trouble." This is the same advice we need to take when trading. When you make a mistake, get out. Don't let your ego push you into bigger losses.

> **Lesson:** *You need to be able to take the 25 percent loss happily. After all, the market has spoken, telling you that this time, on this trade, you have gotten it wrong. Think of it as saving 75 percent, not as losing 25 percent. Most of the time this will be true.*

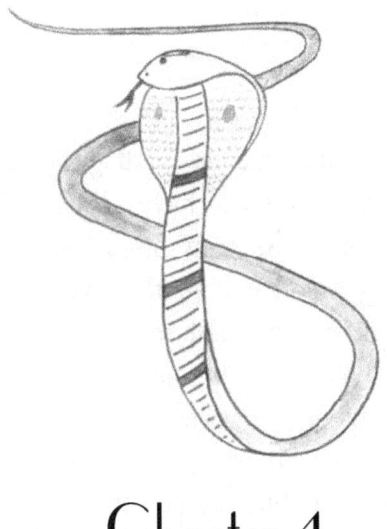

Chapter 4

Evaluating Risk

Well, Do You Feel Lucky, Punk?

In the 1971 movie *Dirty Harry*, directed by Don Siegel and starring the iconic Clint Eastwood in the title role, Clint as Harry foils a bank robbery while downing a hot dog. After cornering the last robber he hasn't yet killed, Harry finds himself in a standoff with him. The robber has a shotgun at arm's length that he can use to kill Harry; but Harry is pointing his pistol at the robber's head. The robber is trying to remember how many shots Harry has taken: if it is six shots, he can pick up the shotgun, kill Harry, and get away; but if Harry only used five shots and he goes for the shotgun, he is a dead man. Harry says, "I know what you're thinking. Did he fire six shots or only five? Well, to tell you the truth, in all this excitement I kind of lost track myself. But since this is a .44 Magnum, the most powerful handgun in the world, and it would blow your head clean off, you've got to ask yourself one question: Do I feel lucky? Well? Do ya, punk?"

***

This is where the robber needs to dispassionately evaluate risk. Not an easy thing to do when you have a gun pointed at your head. Unfortunately, this is where stock investors find themselves today. Do we go all-in and buy stocks as many market mavens are recommending, or do we stay on the sidelines and risk missing the big move up?

Market pundits and stockbrokers continually speak of an investor's risk tolerance, but they never go on to explain what the heck that means. It is not sufficient for an investor to say, "I've always been a risk taker, so my risk tolerance is high; I'm buying the bank stocks and I'm borrowing the money to do it." Nor is it sufficient for another investor to say, "I'm very conservative, so my risk tolerance is low. I'm buying Treasury bills at zero or negative interest rates." This is not the dispassionate evaluation of risk that we need to have in order to avoid the threat of losing our entire investment. I believe that in this example, the conservative investor loading up on Treasuries is taking on as much risk as the risk taker buying the banks on margin.

In fact, I had a short position in Treasuries before the final editing of this book.

In the oil refining business, where I worked for over twenty-five years, the process is to boil gasoline at about 1,000 degrees Fahrenheit. If any air gets into the process or if the process gets out of the pipes— boom! This is a big risk, but it's manageable. I have provided below a risk matrix used to remove emotion from the risk evaluation of inherently risky industrial processes.

The left scale of the matrix is your estimation of the probability of something happening:

- High probability—an outcome is a sure thing

- Medium probability—an outcome is possible, but not inevitable

- Low probability—an outcome is so improbable as to be almost nonexistent

The bottom scale is your estimation of the consequences of the event, if it happens:

- High impact—Armageddon; shifts at McDonald's when you are eighty

- Medium impact—big market losses; postponing retirement awhile

- Low impact—almost no consequences, you make the losses back in a week

Threat Level Risk Matrix

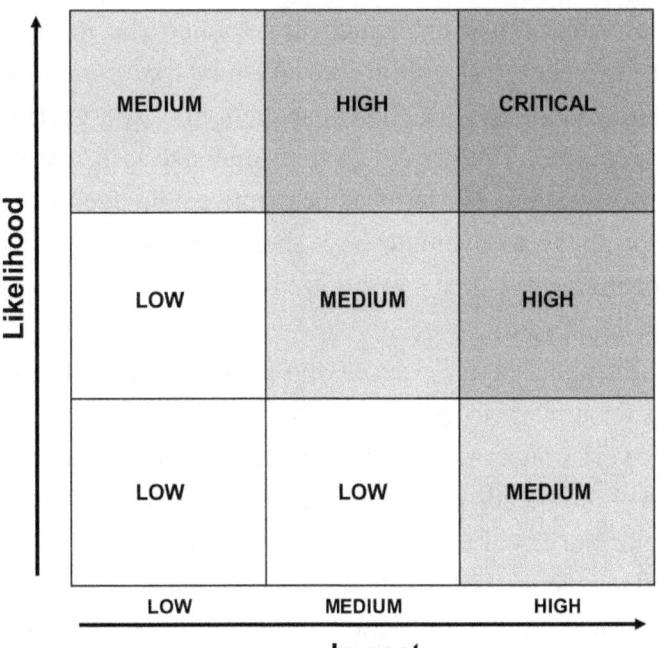

The important thing for each of us in this economy is not our evaluation of the chances of a market recovery or when we think the recovery will begin; the important thing for us to evaluate now is how a wrong guess will affect our ability to survive for the long run. After all, if history is any guide the markets will recover *someday*; we need our capital to survive until then. Money invested in stocks now can appreciate dramatically or it can drift lower for a long, long time. If Warren Buffet loses a bundle, as he did after taking big positions in Goldman Sachs and Bank of America, he is still a billionaire and won't ever need to flip burgers to pay his mortgage. The consequences of his losses are painful but not cataclysmic. He says he can wait five or ten years for his investments to make money, and they are already coming back. Those of us who are not billionaires must evaluate the impact of losses in terms of our current financial situation and our long-term goals.

In my view, if you are twenty-five or thirty years old and have a long-term investment plan like a 401(k), you should continue to dollar-cost average new money into stocks as fast as possible, maximize contributions *right now*—short-term losses now will only make your current contributions worth much more when the markets recover. You're buying cheap. If you are an old guy like me and don't have thirty or forty years to wait, the consequences of short-term losses are much more severe. The impact of the same size loss is very different for the two investors. Those of us near retirement age need to use the risk matrix above to evaluate how short-term losses will affect our ability to achieve our goals. We don't have the time to take risks that may prove cataclysmic.

As an example, take a person who is very close to retirement who is looking for a place to get back into the stock market. However, this investor is very concerned that the market is ready for a 10–15 percent correction—all it needs is for Congress to make a dumb move, like not dealing with the fiscal cliff. A 10 percent decline from 13,000 would bring the Dow Jones Industrial Average to about 11,700. This normal and very typical market correction is enough to wipe us out if we are fully invested without protection. A closer look at the risk matrix may help us to decide what we want to do.

Say, for the sake of this example, that I believe that the likelihood of the market correction is medium.

The impact of our investment options are:

- Nibble a little with a very small investment—low.

- Take a bigger bite with a significant chunk of our savings—medium.

- Go all in with everything, including the kid's college fund—high.

To estimate the threat of our investment options, using our estimated possible outcome—medium—we can use the risk matrix:

- We nibble: The impact of a small investment is low. Using the matrix, the threat is low.

- We take a bigger bite: The impact of investing a significant amount is medium. Using the matrix the threat is medium.

- We go all-in: The impact of risking everything is high. Using the matrix the threat is high.

If I believe that the likelihood of the correction is medium and I put a small amount of money to work in this market, money I can stand to lose, I am knowingly taking on a low threat. The impact of losing the investment is low and the resulting threat is also low. That is my informed choice. If on the other hand I bet my kid's college fund, money I can't afford to lose and still achieve my goals, the impact of losing the investment is high. I am taking on a high threat. These are two very different threats from the same market outcome. And if my assessment of the likelihood of a correction increases to high, the resulting threat levels also increase. The nibble takes on a medium threat, the bigger bite becomes a high threat, and all-in takes us to the critical threat level.

These levels of threat are unacceptable for me to load up my dividend portfolio in the current markets. Small, fast, targeted investments have a low level of threat, so they are still viable while I wait for the market outlook to solidify. If I were the robber in *Dirty Harry* I wouldn't reach for the shotgun just yet. The threat is still too great.

The risk matrix can also be used to evaluate the other side of the coin. Our risk can also be missing the market bottom and not having money at work during an extended upturn. One major oil company calls this risk a "missed profit opportunity." The matrix works the same way when evaluating the risk of not doing something. When evaluating an investment, both the threat of a loss and the threat of a missed opportunity must be balanced. One of our biggest risks is that this market does what the market did after the 1929 crash and bounces along the bottom for twenty-five years.

By the time this book was published the markets had more than doubled since the March 2009 generational bottom.

One way to avoid the risk of owning stocks is simply not to own any; but then we run the risk of missing out on a big market recovery. Another way to offset risk is to buy insurance. Say you own a house; you buy insurance on the house. Own a car? You buy insurance on that car. You have a family; you buy life insurance. You need the insurance because you own the asset insured.

In the stock market one way we can mitigate the risk to our investments is through the use of options:

- As a form of insurance—selling covered calls or buying puts against our stock positions.

- As a way to reduce the amounts we put at risk—buying call spreads instead of the underlying stock.

Both of these strategies will reduce risk, but at the cost of maximum earning potential. Investing is sometimes like football, the important thing is not how many points you have at the end of the game, but only that you have enough points to win.

Mike Ditka, the famous Chicago Bears football coach, has said, "A great team needs to do three things well: Run the ball, stop the run, and have efficient special teams." Trent Dilfer, a retired NFL quarterback and TV commentator, says, "If you have a dominant defense, all you need on offense are four possessions that are optimized by getting points, even field goals."

> **Lesson:** *The point for us traders is, do the basics and don't take chances. We don't need to run up the score to win.*

An old saying the buy-and-hold crowd uses all the time is, "You can't time the market." They say that if you buy and hold, the average return on the stock market over time is about 10 percent per year. They keep repeating that this 10 percent gain is usually made in just ten or fifteen great up days during the year. If you are out of the market when these days hit, you will miss on the entire year. What they always *forget* to say is that the markets have been flat for the last dozen years.

You may not be able to time the market, but you need to be able to see the train wreck coming. Most of my 50 percent beating of the market indexes in 2008 was due to putting almost all my money into cash in March 2007, just before the Shanghai market dropped 9 percent in a single day. I stayed in cash all through 2007 and missed a nice upturn in the markets, but interest rates were very high on cash and I was still making about 3.5 percent on my cash investments. This position was much too conservative for the bull market of 2007, and I missed many opportunities, but it was this position that kept me out of the train wreck of 2008.

Most of my 2008 upside trading performance was due to frenetically trading options and catching a short-term bullish move in techs during the bear market; buying during the January downturn; and selling into the April short-term top. Specifically, I bought Apple at $134 and sold it at $185 and I bought Research in Motion at $114 and sold it at $143. This was a very short-term trade, and very risky. I did protect the trade, and limit my gains, by selling covered calls and buying puts on both stocks—this is a classic "collar" position.

What is a collar? It is a way to trade that limits downside risk. It does that at the cost of upside gains. It is done using stock options. I have often said that if an individual does not understand options, and how they can be utilized to limit losses, that person should not own stocks.

As an example, I will use the Apple trade I did in the first quarter of 2008. I bought Apple stock at $134. Then I immediately sold a call option on Apple several months out. This call option committed me to sell my Apple stock at the strike price of the option—I sold the 195 call option at $14.60, committing myself to sell my Apple stock at $195 in a couple of months. Well, I would have loved to sell the stock at $195; that would have been a 45 percent gain. More importantly, by selling the call and getting the money, my actual risk cost of the stock was reduced: I spent $134 and received $14.60, so the risk cost was $119.84. I couldn't lose money unless the Apple stock price dropped to less than $120 per share.

If you sell the option, as I sold the call, the guy who buys it has the option to exercise the contract. If the price of the stock goes up to the call option strike price, it is 100 percent sure they will "call away" your stock. In my Apple trade that would have been great, considering it would have produced a 45 percent profit. If the stock price does not get up to the contract strike price, the contract will probably expire and just go away—with you keeping the option money. It is important to realize that the term "option" means just that; if you own the option contract, you have the *option* to exercise the contract. If the trade doesn't go your way, you can chose to let the option contract expire without losing any more than what the option initially cost you.

But 2008 was a very scary time. In fact, Apple bottomed out during this down leg at about $102, more than $18 below where my covered call protection stopped working. Lucky for me that the markets were so scary that I wanted even more protection for the trade—I also bought naked put options on Apple.

A put option is similar to a call, but a put option is a contract to sell the underlying stock at some future date. The price of a put option increases as the price of the underlying stock decreases. I bought the right to sell Apple stock at a fixed price, before the big leg down. I bought the put options that had a strike price of $115, just $5 below where my covered call protection broke down. This gave me the right to sell the stock at $115. With the stock at $134, I wouldn't want to do this, of course; but if the stock price dropped below $115, say to $102, I would be very happy to have the right to sell it at $115—a $13 profit.

So as the stock price dropped, the value of the call options I sold decreased and the value of the put options I bought increased in the minds of the people trading them. At the time I built the collar, the cost of the 115 put option was $0.86 because everyone thought the stock was going up and the 115 strike of the put would never be reached. Since I was not buying the put to speculate, but instead for protection on my stock position, it made sense to me. I bought the puts because I had already protected myself against the eventuality of Apple stock dropping to $120 by selling the call options, but I had no protection below $120. By buying the put options, I gave myself protection below $115 and downward. I actually did speculate a little because I also bought naked puts at an even lower strike level, ten times as many puts as number of stocks I owned, but this doesn't change the math of the original collar.

If Apple stock price dropped to zero, the value of the puts would be worth the strike price of $115 at expiration and the calls I sold for $14.60 would expire worthless. So in the worst imaginable case, Armageddon for Apple stock, I would still have $129.60 in option money, a loss on the trade of just $4.40—not counting the naked puts I had bought cheaply at the much lower strike price. When the price of Apple fell, dropping way below $120, the puts were the only thing that kept me in the game. When I believed that the price of Apple stock was low enough, I sold the put option protection for $2.51, a profit of $1.65 or 192 percent for this leg—thus lowering my risk cost of the collar again, from $119.84 to $118.19.

This would have been a great time to buy back the call options I had sold, as they were selling for much, much less than the price at which I had sold them, but I was still scared and still wanted the protection. Looking back as a Monday morning quarterback, I should have bought them back, taken the profit, and sold more calls at a lower strike price. These lower strike calls would have been more expensive because they were closer to the price of the stock. Alternatively, I could have sold the second set of calls further out in time. These contracts would have been more expensive because the time premium portion of option price, the premium, increases with longer dated contracts. Remember that as a seller the higher prices were a good thing.

As I traded it, the price of the Apple stock came back up and as it increased the price of the call options also increased, but at a slower rate than the price of the stock. Remember, I owned the stock but owed the calls. I wanted the price of the stock high and the price of the calls low. With time running down to the contract expiration date, the time premium evaporated, and less people wanted to take the chance, so the call option price increased at a slower rate than the stock price. The spice came out of the calls faster than the increase in the price of the stock could support their price.

When I closed out my Apple collar trade, I bought back the call options at a loss; I bought them back at $17.55. The $14.60 I received from selling the call needs to be subtracted from the buy-back cost, for a total outlay for the call protection, or loss, of $2.95. The profit from one round trip of naked puts was $1.65, so this needs to be subtracted from the total cost of the collar. So the net cost of the collar becomes the cost of the stock ($134) plus the loss on the calls ($2.95) less the gain on the put ($1.65), bringing the overall cost equal to $134 + $2.95 - $1.65 = $135.30. This combination of trades increased my cost of owning the Apple stock to $135.30 a share. Think of the cost of the collar as the cost of insurance. This was all good because I finally sold the stock for $184.

Remember, the stock had decreased to as low as $102 a share. I wasn't forced to sell because the net value of the entire structure of the collar—the stock, the calls sold, and the puts bought—remained relatively constant as the price of the stock dropped.

This may be confusing because of what I have said about reducing my risk cost by selling the call options. I said that by selling the calls, the cost of the stock dropped to $119.84, but this is really the cost of the combined structure of the stock linked to the call contracts. When thinking about the downside, $119.84 was the most I could lose on the stock after selling the calls against it.

As long as someone else owned the right to buy my stock, they owned the calls I sold; I couldn't sell the stock. Therefore the stock and calls sold against it were linked; I needed to buy back the calls before I could sell the stock. The naked puts I bought were free from this entanglement. The overall profit on the collar was $48.70 (36 percent) per share, and I had a lot of shares, with downside protection the entire time. As unbelievable as it may seem, it is almost impossible to lose money with a properly constructed collar. This is the game the big dogs play, so why shouldn't we?

The trade explained above is a simplified version of the collar trade I used to play Apple; in fact, I sold and bought back call options several times and bought and sold back put options several times. My actual profit on the trades I used during the collar ended up just below 35 percent including sales commissions. Had I just let the options run to expiration, not buying back the calls, my AAPL stock would have been "called away" and the gain on the trade would have been about 50 percent. But hindsight is 20:20.

The profit on my Research in Motion collar wound up a bit lower (about 20 percent) because I took the protection off later than I should have. This type of hedging is the kind of thing the hedge funds were originally formed to do, but they got greedy—sure death in the markets. They got to the point where the idea of losing upside potential was so unpalatable that they didn't put on the rational downside protection. It is interesting to note that the collar strategy is so sure to make money that

Bernie Madoff used it to explain to his investors why he never lost. You do need to place the trades, though.

One last note for trading in a bear market: the collar trade is not as attractive during a bear market as it is during a bull upswing. This is because the overall market pessimism changes the pricing of the options: call options are cheaper (less money if you sell a covered call) and put options are more expensive (more costly to buy put protection). Although the profits are much lower, the collar trade still works. I am looking forward to a time, maybe a year or two out, when the bull market returns.

As discussed at length in chapter 3, there is a very human emotional aspect to investing. Every time I take on a position and it hits really big, I think to myself, "I wish I had trusted my intuition more; I could have really backed up the truck." Yet every time I'm wrong, but I have limited my losses by not backing up the truck, I think, "I really had good instincts on that one." If the proper options protection is unemotionally utilized, gains are limited, but losses are too.

Fine, so the markets and trading are emotional. How can we manage to not let our emotions control us? How can we coldly and unemotionally evaluate the markets? One tool used by traders is technical analysis, the use of charts to predict the future. This is a giant field and I am no expert. There is a good book listed in this book's bibliography that can get an interested reader started in this murky world of seeing things where others see nothing. I do use a few of the technicians' tools: Bollinger Bands, trend lines, and support and resistance lines.

I draw very accurate support and resistance lines, probably because we needed to know how to do this when I was a chemist before the computer age. It was part of my education. I also can see and draw a trading channel that is uncannily accurate. I do need to trust this more and trade more appropriately. I also have an intuitive feel for Bollinger Bands as we used statistical process control and control charts when monitoring processes in refineries.

I found a detailed explanation of how traders use Bollinger Bands at Technitrader.com. I have included it at the end of this book, in the "Useful Stuff" section. Bollinger Bands are a small subset of statistical process control (SPC)—the process used in industry to optimize their processes and profits while minimizing their risks.

I have also provided in the "Useful Stuff" section a detailed article on SPC I found on Wikipedia. In industry, SPC is the bible for controlling variables in a process. The first time I was exposed to SPC, it was like a hood had been removed from over my head. I could finally see. I included SPC into every program I built for my customers. It not only helped management improve the bottom line—and safety—but also helped the blue-collar guys by showing that problems were not always due to their mistakes or sloth. When I watch a stock's trend line or check a stock's Bollinger Bands I always refer back to my use of SPC in industry.

Finally, when discussing investment risks and the methods of mitigating them, the use of stock and index options must be covered. This is a huge subject, much larger than the Apple example I have provided above. In the next chapter I will go into much more detail about how options can be used:

- As insurance against loss.

- As a low-cost way to mirror the gains of strong stocks, exchange-traded funds, and the overall markets.

- As a way to profit from the declines of weak markets and securities.

Chapter 5

The Options Market

War, or the Promise of Promise

In 1970 the movie *Patton* was released and my father—who fought with Patton as a member of Third Army, Fourth Armored Division, and Thirty-Seventh Tank Battalion (who broke through to Bastogne)—was ecstatic. Directed by Franklin J. Schaffner, the film won eight Academy Awards, including the award for best picture. Perfect casting made the screenplay, written by Francis Ford Coppola and Edmund H. North, come alive. Patton was played by George C. Scott, Omar Bradley by Karl Malden, and the British general Bernard Montgomery—whom my father called the "ferocious rabbit"—was ably portrayed by Michael Bates. The surprisingly admirable German field marshal Erwin Rommel was played by Karl Michael Vogler. The movie opens with Patton giving a speech to his men, a real speech given in England on May 31, 1944, standing in front a gigantic American flag that fills the screen behind him, ivory pistols at his side: "Now I want you to remember that no bastard ever won a war by dying for his country. He won it by making the other poor dumb bastard die for his country."

***

No statement could apply better to the options market—options are a zero-sum game, for every winner there is a loser. It is war. It is the option trader's job to make "the other poor dumb bastard" lose his money.

Patton also said, "A good solution applied with vigor *now* is better than a perfect solution ten minutes later." He could have been an options trader. This is a much better way of stating my first rule of trading: don't be slow.

Stocks trade on emotion, being only loosely related to the underlying businesses, and options are only remotely related to the underlying stocks. You might say that options are the promise of the promise of the underlying business. If you want to be an investor, you must search your personality to discover whether you are inherently a bull or a bear. It doesn't matter which, but you need to know your tendencies. I am bullish by nature. This makes me do much better in a bull market than in a bear market. The first year of the market decline was the biggest bear market in modern history, which put my trading tendencies at a huge disadvantage. During that year I was up about 17 percent in realized and unrealized gains. This beats the performance of the market indexes by over 50 percent, and this is during a market that did not favor my natural tendencies.

In November 2008 one of my newsletter subscribers, a highly educated and skilled medical professional, asked me if I was a day trader. I had to think about it for a second. "I do it every day, so I suppose I am," I had to answer. Throughout my investing career I have prided myself on my ability to see the big global trends. This is my natural method of investment; a slow, methodical process. The markets during 2008, however, made long-term, trend-based investments difficult and very painful. The market in those days made us all day traders—if we wanted to make a little money in the treacherous environment. My medical colleague also asked if I could explain to a very busy person just what the heck stock options are and how they work. This will take some time.

Options. A stock option is a contract that gives the owner the right to force a trade in the future. The option contract defines the stock, the price, and the last date the owner can choose to force the trade. The contract owner has the "option" to force the trade or not.

Call Option. A stock "call" option gives you, the owner, the right to *buy* a stock at a specific price for a limited time. The name comes from the old days when the option owner would find the unfortunate guy who had sold the contract and "call" him over to produce the stock he had agreed to sell at a price lower than it was currently trading. The Dec 50 call option, for example, is a contract giving the right to buy the stock at $50 at any time until the expiration date, the third Friday in December. The price of a call option has two parts: the *intrinsic value* and the *time premium.*

Put Option. A stock "put" option gives you, the owner, the right to *sell* a stock at a specific price for a limited time. The name comes from when the option owner would walk across the trading floor and "put" the stock to the poor guy who had to buy it at a price higher than its value at that moment. The Dec 50 put option is a contract giving the right to sell the stock at $50 at any time until the expiration date, the third Friday in December. As with a call option, the price of a put option has two parts: the *intrinsic value* and the *time premium.*

Option Premium. The premium of an option is the price that is paid for it. Since each option contract is for one hundred shares of the underlying security, the total cost of the option contract is one hundred times the premium. The premium has two parts: the *intrinsic value* and the *time premium.*

If a stock is trading at $101, the call option with a $100 strike has an intrinsic value of $1. The call is $1 "in the money"—that is, if the stock is assigned to you at $100 and you can sell it for $101, you make a buck. In the same case, if the call contracts are trading at $3, the extra $2 is the time premium. The time premium of an option, what I sometimes call the "spice," is the portion of the option selling price above the intrinsic value of the contract. The option buyer is paying for the time to let the stock go up—it may go up much more than the $2 extra paid for the contract.

If a stock is at $98, the call option with a $100 Strike is $2 "out of the money." Even so, the call option with the $100 strike may still trade at $3, even though the strike is above the stock price. Since the call contract, in this case, has zero intrinsic value, the $3 paid for the contract is all time premium. If you bought the contract at $3 and exercised it at $100 when the stock was at $98 you would lose $2 buying the stock and you would still be out the $3 you paid for the right to do it. You would lose five bucks. As the time to the expiration date gets closer the chances that the stock price will reach the strike price diminish, and the time premium decreases.

The intrinsic value of a call option is the *price of the stock minus the strike price* (this stops at zero; it doesn't go negative). Say a stock traded at $45 when the Dec 50 call was at $4 (this actually happened to me when I was trading Research in Motion). The intrinsic value ($45–50) of the option was zero—if the stock was $51, the intrinsic value would be $1. The time premium is the price of the call option minus the Intrinsic Value ($4 - $0 = $4). Therefore, the example Dec 50 call has a time premium of $4. This is important because typically as the time on the contact decreases, so does the time premium. This is generally true, but big moves in the stock or in the overall market increase volatility and can reverse this trend. At the market close on expiration day, the time premium goes to zero.

The intrinsic value of a put option is the *strike price minus the price of the stock* (this stops at zero; it doesn't go negative). Say a stock traded at $55 when the Dec 50 put was at $4. The intrinsic value ($50–55) of the option is zero—if the stock is at $49, the intrinsic value would be $1. The time premium is the price of the put option minus the intrinsic value. Therefore, the Dec 50 put in this example has a time premium, or spice, of $4.00. This is important because as the time on the contact decreases, so does the time premium, unless there is an increase in stock market volatility. At the market close on expiration day, the time premium goes to zero.

Since the seller of the call option is giving up some rights to the stock, they will want some money for compensation—the price of the call option. When I sold my position in Research in Motion (RIMM) at $45.30, the Dec 50 call was trading at $4.25. Why would someone pay $4.25 for the right to purchase a $45 stock for $50? They won't break even until the stock trades above $54.25—what they paid for the option plus what they will pay for the stock. If they believe the stock is going this high, why wouldn't they just buy the stock for $45? After all, if the stock doesn't go above $50, they won't buy it and they will lose the $4.25 they paid for the rights to buy. There are many reasons, but let's just discuss *leverage* and *protection*.

Leverage. Say I buy the stock at $45 and it goes up to $50. I have made $5, or 11.1 percent profit. If I buy the call option for $4.25 and the underlying stock price increases to $50, the price of the call option will increase too, but not as much, probably to about $8.00. The option trade yields only $3.75 per share, but this is a profit of 88.2 percent.

Protection. In the last chapter I used my Apple collar trade at the height of the crisis as an example of how options can be used as protection. There are other ways they are valuable. Say I'm a hedge fund manager and I believe that the price of RIMM is going to go down. I might sell short. Selling short is another type of trade that is probably not a good idea for the typical retirement plan, but please accept that a stock can be sold by someone who doesn't own it, for a price below the current trading price. The seller pockets the money and can make other investments with it. If the stock price drops below where the seller sold it, he or she buys back the short position and makes the additional difference on the short. If the price does not drop, these sorts of sellers lose the shirts off their backs because they need to buy the stock at the market to honor their contracts, whatever the price. But if they also own contracts that allow them to buy the stock at a set price—a call—the risk is defined.

Originally, hedge funds were touted as a way investors could share the brilliance of fund managers who knew how to "hedge" their bets, to limit any chance of a loss. Although they didn't do such a good job of that during the crash! If they sell the stock short—say they sell RIMM at $44 a share when it is trading at $45—they *can* take the risk that the stock will rise without additional protection, but this position would not be hedged. They sell stock they don't own and they don't own an option to buy at a fixed price for protection. The potential losses, if they are wrong, are infinite. But they *may* choose to protect themselves.

One way they can protect themselves is to buy corresponding call options. If they buy the right to buy the stock at $50 (the Dec 50 call) for $4.25, they can only lose $10.25 per share—they have the $44 they made from the short sale, less the $4.25 cost of the call, less the $50 they will pay for the stock if they are forced to cover their short ($44 - $4.25 - $50 = -$10.25). This sounds like a big loss, but if the stock went to $100 and they were obligated to produce the stock they sold, they would lose $60 per share. If the stock goes back to where it was in April 2008, $145 per share, they lose $101 per share. To complete their protection, they could take on other, opposite positions; they could sell put options—another discussion completely—to protect themselves from the $10.25 loss, but let's not make this even more complicated.

Now, if the $45 call was trading at $6.40, they could buy this call for protection instead of the Dec 50, and their maximum loss would be $7.40 per share. Their potential profit, if the price of the stock went to, say, $5, is $32.60 per share: the difference on the short ($44 - $5 = $39) less the price of the protection ($39 - $6.40 = $32.60).

The phrase "put it to" someone, I believe comes from a put option. If you own the put, you have the right to make someone buy a stock at a defined price, even if the market price is way, way lower than that price. They will need to buy the stock at your price and eat the difference—you really "put it to them."

> **Lesson:** Remember: *the options market is a zero-sum game; for every winner there is a loser.*

Here is one more important, and confusing, point about options. I'll stay with call options. A call option is a contract that gives the owner the right to buy a stock at a specific price within a specific time. If I buy the Dec 50 call at $4.25, I have the right to force the sale of the stock at $50 at any time until the contract expiration date. But there is another, opposite, side to the contract. Somebody is going to be obligated to sell you the stock at $50. This somebody is called the contract "writer." When I sell the Dec 50 call, I write the contract. I immediately get the $4.25 per share, but if the price of the stock increases to above $50, the guy who bought the call option will want my stock and he will get it. It is *assigned* and sells automatically; I get the $50 and pay the sales commission. The only way to avoid selling my stock at $50 is to buy back, at a loss, the call option I wrote. If the stock is above $50 and the call is at $8, I would lose $3.75 to buy the call back.

If the stock price does not move higher than the call option strike price on expiration day, no contract execution happens, the stock is not assigned, and the call option expires worthless. This is a good thing if you wrote the contract, but it is a bad thing if you bought the contract. If I sell the call, I am short—I owe—a contract that gives the right to buy. If I buy the call, I am long—I own—a contract that gives the right to buy.

Spice. There is an old market saying that goes something like this: "We don't care where a stock has been, we only care where it is going." But in the options market this saying is wrong. It matters very much how a stock got to where it is. Where the stock has been and how fast it has moved from there are the most important things. They are the parameters that shape the market emotion—the spice.

In the options market there is a critical yet nebulous phenomenon I like to refer to as the spice. The time premium is defined by the volatility in the stock and the time left on the contract. I use the term spice to refer to the portion of the time premium that reflects the market's feeling of well-being and the confidence level of the global trading gestalt. Although it is a portion of the time premium, the spice flows with the excitement of the trade; it is the intangible, human, emotional part of the price. The spice flows not only from where a stock is and from where it was and how fast has it changed position but also from the hope and fear component. Many times I have watched the price of a call option tumble while the price of the stock moved upward, the spice pouring out of the value of the option as the emotions of the market suck the spice, the volatility, from the price. The value of the option's spice seems to be more dependent on the second derivative of the stock price—the speed of change of the price, more than the change of price.

A $200 stock that has been at about $200 for a while won't have much emotional interest (or spice). There will still be a time premium, but if the same stock got to the same price in a hurry, the options will be very spicy; the time premium will be larger by the amount of emotion (or spice).

The time premium is the confidence and probability component of an option's price; the sum of each individual trader's personal emotional state will define and frame the value of the spice within it. If you buy a call option with a strike price of $100 and the stock is already trading at the $100 strike price, then the amount paid for the option is all time premium—there is no intrinsic value. If the price paid for each call option is $10, then the time premium is $10. If the option contract expires in twelve months, this time premium, though large, may seem reasonable—$10 may be a fair price. Contract prices this far out in time change slowly, if at all. The spice is very small. But if the contract expires in four days, a $10 time premium would seem to be a very high price. The spice is very large. What I call the spice is the sentiment support under the option time premium.

> **Lesson:** *Options with less than thirty days left before expiration should not be bought to hold more than a few days. Make it or break it today.*

Some people think that trading options is just too dangerous or too difficult. In fact, I believe that if you don't understand and utilize stock options, you probably should not be buying and selling stocks at all. There are plenty of mutual funds and exchange traded funds out there that may work better for you; although even these may be huge losers if they are not properly hedged.

When it comes to doing something that is difficult, I'm reminded of the old golfer's joke about the one iron. A guy shanks a one-iron shot into the weeds and begins to curse golf, the world, and all God's creation, waving his one iron blasphemously toward the heavens. Suddenly a bolt of lightning explodes from the clear blue sky, roaring as it flashes onto the fairway nearby, missing the blasphemer by ten yards.

"See," says the golfer to his partner, the club hanging calmly at his side. "Even God can't hit a one iron."

Below I have listed some of the basic option trades that can help you increase profit with leverage or protect your conservative positions with option hedging. These relatively simple option strategies are easily understood and can be used in day-to-day trading. There are many, many more strategies that are much more complicated that I believe should be left to the professionals. I have listed a great book about options in the bibliography; if you think you need to get more complicated than these basic trades, you'd better buy some books on options and bone up before attempting the more complicated ones.

Writing a covered call. This is a protection or optimization strategy. The owner of a stock sells, or writes, a call option against the stock. If the stock drops, the price of the call also drops and the owner can buy back the call at a lower price. This protects the stock owner from a drop in the stock price equal to the amount received for the call. If the price of the stock increases, the stock owner only makes profit up to where the call contract requires him to sell. A call that is in the money—the stock price is higher than the strike price—will always be executed and the call seller's stock will be "called away" on expiration day. If the stock price is flat, an out-of-the-money option expires worthless, and the premium earned increases the yield of the trade. Writing or selling a naked call—that is, you don't own the stock—is extremely dangerous. The potential losses are mathematically infinite. There is no place in my investing philosophy for this risky trade.

Writing a collar. A collar is the same as a covered call, except that a naked put is also purchased, usually with the money received from writing the call. The covered call can only protect the stock down to the strike price of the call written. The naked put will continue to increase in value all the way down to a stock price of zero. A properly structured collar can't lose money. You can have your stock called away, but the net of the trade will be even or in the money. I collared Apple and Research in Motion in 2008 for nice wins—the downside is that I was doing this when Apple was trading at below $150. Sure wish I stilled owned some $135 Apple in 2012.

The naked call. A trader buys a call option because he or she believes the stock is moving up. If the stock price increases, the call option can be sold at a higher price than where it was bought. If the stock price falls, the call loses value. If the stock price is lower than the call strike price at expiration, and the trader does not buy back the call at a loss, the contract expires worthless, and the trader loses the entire investment. The trader's maximum loss is the amount paid for the call. The call buyer is not obligated in any way; however, if the stock moves above the strike price of the call, making the trader money, and the call is not sold to close the position, the contract may be automatically exercised and the stock purchased in the trader's account. A trader needs to know the policies of his brokerage house, but it is usually best to close out a winning options trade unless you want the contract exercised.

The bullish call spread. This strategy is about as safe as option speculation gets. A trader believes a stock is moving up, but the price of a naked call is too high. He or she buys a call close to or lower than the stock trading price and simultaneously sells a call with a strike further away, higher than, the stock price. Say the stock is at $50; the trader may buy the $48 strike and sell the $52 strike, lowering the cost of the trade. Both options will increase if the stock price increases, but the lower strike will increase more.

The naked put. Puts have a darkness to them because it is a bet that the underlying stock is going to go down. A trader buys a put option because he or she believes the stock is moving down. If the stock price decreases, the put option can be sold at a price than higher where it was bought. If the stock moves up, the put loses value. If the stock price is higher than the put strike price at expiration, and the trader does not buy back the put at a loss, the contact expires worthless, and the trader loses the entire investment. The trader's maximum loss is the amount paid for the put initially. The put buyer is not obligated in any way; however, if the stock moves below the strike, making the trader money, and the put is not sold to close the position, the contract may be automatically exercised by the trader's broker and the stock sold in the trader's account. A trader needs to know the policies of his or her brokerage house, but it is usually best to close out a winning options trade unless you want the contract exercised.

The bearish put spread. As far as puts go, buying a put spread is about as safe as you can go. A trader believes a stock is moving down, but the price of a naked put is too high. He or she buys a put close to or higher than the stock's trading price and simultaneously sells a put with a strike further away, lower than, the stock price. Say the stock is at $50; the trader may buy the $52 strike and sell the $48 strike. Both options will increase if the stock price decreases, but the higher strike will increase more.

Writing a naked put. The potential losses built into this trade are equal to the strike price sold. The only reason for you to use this strategy is that you want to buy the stock anyway; you sell the put at a strike price lower than where you can buy the stock, and only two things can happen: the stock goes down and you buy the stock at the lower strike price or the stock goes up and you pocket the option premium. If you write the put, you get the premium, yours to keep. If the stock goes up, you keep the premium and can buy the stock you want at a higher price than when you sold the put without losing out on the gain or you could buy back the put at a cheaper price. But if the stock goes down, look out! You need to buy back the put fast or risk huge losses if you get the stock put to you at a price much higher than where it is trading on expiration day (as happened to me when I wrote puts on BP). I have used this strategy a few times, and it is not one I'd recommend to the beginner.

The straddle. An option straddle is entered when a trader simultaneously buys both calls and puts on the same stock. If the stock increases indefinitely, the calls have infinite upside and the puts can only lose as much as they initially cost, so theoretically the trade has infinite upside. If the stock goes to zero, the calls can lose only as much as they initially cost, while the puts can only make as much as the stock can go down. So in the case of a down move in the stock, profit for the trade is limited to the price of the stock less the costs of the options. If the stock does nothing, both the calls and the puts could expire worthless. A straddle position is great for keeping trader emotions at bay.

In a flat market, which might produce the last possibility above—the stock does nothing—a speculator can write both the call and the put. If the stock goes up, the call will also increase in price, but the put will decrease. When the put stops decreasing the write straddle will really start losing money, so the call would be repurchased to avoid huge losses. If as originally expected the stock doesn't move much and doesn't pass either strike price, the trader keeps both option premiums received.

The leap. This is the same as an option, but instead of a lifetime measured in months a leap has an expiration date that extends out beyond a year.

Approximate Profit or Loss for Basic Strategies

TYPE OF OPTION	POTENTIAL PROFIT	POTENTIAL LOSS
Naked call	Infinite	Your cost
Naked put	Strike price	Your cost
Covered call	Strike price - stock price + call price	Stock price - call price
Collar	Same as covered call - put price	Call price - put price
Call spread	Limited by strikes	Limited by strikes
Put spread	Limited by strikes	Limited by strikes
Straddle	Infinite	Your cost

If you have call options that are deeply in the money and they are nearing expiration, you may want to consider waiting for the deadline. If they stay in the money, you will buy the stock at a discount equal to the amount the calls are in the money. If you don't want to own the stock you can sell it right away. This will usually save you a lot in trading commissions. However, the *if* is a big one. I have tried to do this, and on several occasions the stock price broke down minutes before expiration and I was out the profits I had just a few hours before.

> **Lesson:** *If you want to own the stock anyway, let in-the-money calls expire. Otherwise don't wait; take the profits before the last few days of the contract and the noise that surrounds the expiration.*

Option prices, both for puts and calls, decrease as the distance between the strike price and the current stock price increases. The further away from the current stock price the option strikes, the lower the probability that the strike will be reached, so the price people will pay is lower. Strikes closer to the current stock price have a higher probability of being reached, so they are more valuable. Once the strike has been reached the option is in the money and will increase at almost the same rate, dollar for dollar, with any further increase in the stock price.

In Randall Wallace's 2002 film *We Were Soldiers*, starring Mel Gibson as US lieutenant colonel Hal Moore and Don Duong as the North Vietnamese commander Nguyen Huu An, the story of the bloody Battle of la Drang is dramatized. Just before the final assault by the North Vietnamese forces, Nguyen coaches his troops on how to avoid the devastating American artillery fire. He tells them they need to stay in close: "Grab them by the belt buckle and hang on."

> **Lesson:** *When trading options, a flea needs to fight the battle like the North Vietnamese—staying in close to avoid the artillery. "Grab them by the belt buckle and hang on." In the options market this means buying fewer options nearer the trading price of the underlying security, rather than more options further out.*

When considering the differences between an option spread and naked options, it is usually the high price of the options that makes the spread win out. If the direction of the stock goes your way, the naked option will always make more money. But the high cost of the options makes the spread position more desirable, even with its limited upside, because of the lower initial cost and the lower risk if the stock price goes against you. This is especially true if you "grab them by the belt buckle" and buy near the price of the underlying stock. The high cost of each leg (usually above $10) of the trade prevents me and other fleas from trading them naked. The altitude below becomes terrifyingly high when you are naked. One hundred contracts at $10 costs $100,000. But the high cost of each leg is a benefit to the spread owner; it provides downside insurance. In the case of a call spread, if each leg goes down by 50 percent—as they will if the stock drops $10 or $15—the value of the spread will stay almost the same, allowing the spread owner to sell or otherwise reevaluate the spread.

Top Gun is the 1986 air-combat action film directed by Tony Scott and produced by Don Simpson and Jerry Bruckheimer. After Maverick (played by Tom Cruise) and Goose (played by Anthony Edwards) get their dream assignments to the navy's best dogfighting school in San Diego, they are pitted against their instructors, played by Tom Skerritt and Michael Ironside. For safety, the training mission has an artificial hard deck well above the ground; during the mission the hard deck will be considered the ground—if they fly below it, they are "dead."

When I buy a spread position, I want one with a lot of air below it, lots of room to go down to what I would call the hard deck. When you price options close to the trading price, especially on a volatile stock, the prices are very high. It is too expensive, and risky, to buy naked options. But the high prices make a spread attractive. In a call spread, if the stock price goes down, both the option you buy (closer to the stock price) and the option you sell (further away from the stock price) will go down, but the option with the lower strike, the one you own, will go down less. What I mean by "lots of air below" concerns the phenomenon of price convergence. Still using the call spread example, the prices of the two options will converge as the stock price drops; when the option prices converge, the value of the spread decreases. If the options were initially too cheap, they won't have room to go down before the converging difference in price causes the spread to lose money. The hard deck is the point where the two options are essentially the same price. And the value of the spread is zero.

If you put on a call spread with plenty of air below, the value of both contracts will go down as the price of the stock drops, but since the option you own goes down slower than the option you are short, you have time to trade; you won't immediately get killed. If you were playing naked options, you would be in big trouble.

> **Lesson:** *Options spreads are options light. Everything about them is slower and lower: the speed, the change, the cost, and the profit.*

When I was in college my summer job was at an army base in the Mojave Desert. One of my jobs was to help the range crew mark duds on the firing ranges. The guys in the range crew were…how can I say this delicately?…heavy drinkers—no delicate way, I guess. One Saturday, after loading our trucks up with cases of beer and quarts of scotch, we went out into the desert to mark duds. While we were out on a range that we thought was inactive, one where the Top Gun guys flew, a flight of F-4 Phantoms from the naval weapons station that abutted the army base flew over. We were out on a dry lake bed in our very, very slow ten-wheel-drive trucks and looked very much like the derelict vehicles the jets had come to strafe. But the pilots were good and took a slow pass to check us out before blowing us up. As we scurried up out of the lake and into the hills, the radio screamed frantically, "That range is live. Repeat, the range is live!" What did I know? I was just a college kid with a ponytail. A few years later, most of the range crew was blown up while disposing of some duds. It was a tremendous tragedy for them, their families, friends and everyone who worked at the sprawling desert facility.

Lesson: *Don't mark duds, or trade options, if you are mentally or emotionally compromised.*

Buying, or selling, close to the trading price is also important for covered call selling, though it isn't as black and white. I wanted to protect my position in Agnico-Eagle Mines (AEM), a Canadian gold miner, by selling the calls against the stock. I wanted to do this because the trend in gold had been gradually taking all the gold mining companies down with it. I had already made two covered call round trips and had made money on each trip. I wanted to keep the protection on, but I got greedy and waited for the perfect price to sell. When the decrease in the price of gold accelerated, I was caught without the wise protection.

On October 11, 2011, AEM closed at $58.31. The Jan 67.50 calls were at $2.80 and the Jan 70 calls were at $2.10. Having an innate greedy nature I wanted to sell the Jan 70s at $2.50, so I held out for that price.

Well, the stock trended lower with the price of gold, and by October 17, a week later, the stock was at $57.55, the Jan 67.50s were at $1.61 and the Jan 70s were at $1.18.

Comparison of Covered Call Pricing for AEM

DATES & VALUES	AEM STOCK	PRICE OF JAN 67.50 CALLS	PRICE OF JAN 70 CALLS
10/11/11	$58.31	$2.80	$2.10
10/17/11	$57.55	$1.61	$1.18
Gain or loss	-$0.76	+$1.19	+$0.92
Percent gain or loss	-1.3 percent	+ 43 percent	+ 44 percent

The total return for the covered call position, the net of the stock, and the calls sold would have been:

For the Jan 67.50s = $1.19 - $0.76 = Positive $0.43, or 0.7 percent based on the stock price.

For the Jan 70s = $0.92 - $0.76 = Positive $0.16, or 0.3 percent based on the stock price.

A difference in performance of less than half a percent is insignificant when compared to the price of the underlying stock. I was just being penny-wise and pound-foolish. But let's look at the what-if scenario—that I had been able to sell the Jan 70s at my desired price of $2.50. The total return for this covered call position would have been: $2.50 - $1.18 = $1.32, or 2.3 percent based on the original price of the stock. This looks like it is a much better trade, but is it really? The Jan 67.50s trade did the job of a covered call: it protected the stock from a sudden decline, much as insurance protects your house or your car. The Jan 70s trade that was available would have made slightly more, but it was more speculative.

Here is the kicker. The Jan 70s trade I wanted, the greedy one I waited for in vain, kept me from buying *any* covered call protection. While I was looking for the perfect trade with the perfect price, reality smacked my unprotected stock.

On October 18, 2011, AEM reported that one of its most productive mines, the GoldEx mine, had flooded, and there was little chance the company could bring it back into operation. At this point I sure wished that I had some of the Jan 67.50 covered call protection. On October 20, the stock closed at $44 a share, down $14.31 or 24.5 percent. And I had no protection.

> **Lesson:** *When you need protection, lay it on. Don't try to get the last few cents in pricing. Or using the age-old saying, "Don't be penny-wise and pound-foolish."*

The Jan 67.50s closed at $0.30 on October 19 and less than a quarter on the October 20, and eventually would expire worthless. The drop from $2.80 to $0.25 is a 92 percent gain! Pretty good as a naked option play, but totally inadequate when compared to the $14.31 drop in the underlying stock. Covered call protection is not enough for an unexpected and precipitous drop. The only way to protect against an act of nature—or corporate idiocy—that blows away the existing trend is to have the ultimate form of option protection: the collar.

> **Lesson:** *The big AEM lesson is the same as the BP lesson. Sell at first sign of an act of nature that negatively affects the stock. Take the immediate loss; it will be smaller than if you wait.*

If you sell calls that are out of the money—that is, with a strike price higher than where the stock is trading at the time—you may *not* protect the stock gains you are trying to protect. This is because the amount you will receive will be relatively small compared to the amount the stock may drop. The positive thing is if the stock goes up, you will do much better because your call-away price is higher. If you sell calls that are in the money—that is, with a strike price lower than where the stock is trading at the time—your downside protection will be relatively large. The negative thing is if the stock goes up, your profit will be limited by low call-away price.

As an example, let's say you have two hundred shares of a stock you purchased at $90 and it has moved up to $100; you are already ahead by $10 and you want to protect that gain. Call A has a strike of $110 and costs $1; call B has a strike of $90 and costs $11. For this example I'll assign each the same time premium of $1. You sell (or write) one contract at each of the strikes; each contract is for one hundred shares. So you receive into your account 100 x $1 = $100 for selling call A and 100 x $11 = $1,100 for call B. This is your money now. The other guy owns the right to buy your stock at the specified strike price. So how do the two contracts compare?

The Stock Increases to $110* and You Get Called Away

STOCK GOES UP TO $110	CALL A, THE $110 STRIKE	CALL B, THE $90 STRIKE	NO CALLS SOLD
Stock buy price	$90	$90	$90
Stock sell price	$110	$90	$110
Received for call	$1	$11	$0
Total return	**$21**	**$11**	**$20**

*The stock is $20 above purchase price and $10 above where protection laid on.

These gains are artificially huge, but they make the numbers of the example easy to follow. *I wish we had moves like this all the time, but we don't.* In both cases the calls move in the money. You will be called away on both contracts—that is, your broker will sell one hundred shares at $90 to comply with call contract A and one hundred shares at $110 to comply with call contract B. You could buy back the contracts, but that is almost never a good idea when the stock moves this much.

If the stock goes up to $110, calls at both strikes will go up. For simplicity in this example, I'll say they both go up by the amount the stock went up: $10. The call with the $110 strike will go to $11 and the call with the $90 strike will go to $21; both have become too expensive to buy back.

The Stock Slowly Decreases below $90* and Calls Expire

STOCK GOES DOWN TO $90	CALL A, $110 STRIKE	CALL B, $90 STRIKE	NO CALLS SOLD
Stock buy price	$90	$90	$90
Stock trading price	$89	$89	$89
Received for call	$1	$11	$0
Total return	**$0**	**$10**	**−$1**

*The stock is $1 below purchase price and $11 lower than where protection was laid on.

If the stock price slowly moves to just below where you bought it at $90, at the end of the contract period the holders of the call contracts will let them expire worthless. Why buy a stock at $90 or $110 through the call contracts when you can buy it at $89 in the open market? Since the contract period is almost finished, the time premiums have all but gone away. You might choose to let the contracts expire or you might buy them back cheaply just before expiration.

In the case of a slow decline back to below your stock buy price, contract B provided much more downside protection. You still have all the profit from when the stock was at $100. But after the calls expire worthless and you pocket the premiums, you are once again left without protection. You will need to repeat the process of writing calls against your stock, or possibly buying puts. Just remember: don't be greedy or slow; get the protection.

Sometimes it does make sense to buy back the call protection. Say the stock goes down and the call price you have sold moves down radically, but the time left on the contract is long. Why wait for conditions to reverse against you? You can buy back your protection, make a big profit, and sit tight, or you could move your protection to a lower strike price by selling another set of calls against your stock position.

The Stock Quickly Decreases Far below $90*

STOCK GOES DOWN TO $80	CALL A, $110 STRIKE	CALL B, $90 STRIKE	NO CALLS SOLD
Stock buy price	$90	$90	$90
Stock trading price	$80	$80	$80
Received for call	$1	$11	$0
Total return	–$9	$1	–$10

*Stock is $10 below purchase price and $20 below where protection laid on.

In the final possibility I discuss, shown as a quick decline in the stock price to a level well below the stock purchase price, the protection has become totally inadequate. Contract A has really done nothing to protect the stock and has probably been bid near $0.05 for some time. Contract B has barely kept the trade even and depending on the market volatility it may also be trading at almost nothing. Since the decline in the stock price has been quick, there may still be a lot of time left on the call contracts—they need to be bought back at these low levels. The covered calls have done all they can do. Close them out and reevaluate. Being short worthless covered calls for the duration of the contract period is worse than being without protection. If the stock continues downward, the calls won't help. If the stock moves back up, the calls will become more expensive to repurchase, depriving the stock owner the benefit of the move back up in the stock. While short the worthless call contracts your hands are tied: you can't sell the stock outright, and new covered calls can't be written on the stock until you close out the old ones.

A higher strike call has the potential to make you more if the stock price increases, but it has little downside protection. A lower strike call will make less if the stock price goes up, but it provides much more downside protection. This is the choice that needs to be made when selecting which contract to write. There is one more thing you could have done. You could have sold the stock at $100 and booked the $10 profit. These days buying and selling stock is cheap. Generally the commissions you will pay on buying and selling options will be significantly higher than the commissions paid for buying and selling stock.

So far my discussion of options has been about option contracts with underlying securities of corporate common stock. But these days there are many more kinds of options than simple stock options; I would be remiss if I didn't mention some of the most important.

Index options. The Chicago Board of Exchange provides a marketplace for traders to buy and sell options on many of the familiar indexes used to track the markets. These option contracts use index funds as the underlying equity. Index funds are carefully structured to mirror the performance of a major market benchmark by holding the same securities. Index funds have been structured to track every index from the very familiar, including the S&P 500, the Dow Jones Industrial Average, and the NASDAQ Composite to relatively obscure indexes like the US Bond Index, the US Real Estate Index, and the California Municipal Bond Index. Most, if not all, of these funds have options associated with them and many, many more sector indexes exist that have options traded based on them. These contracts give the owner the opportunity to control a tiny part of every major stock in these indexes or sectors.

Exchange-traded fund options. An exchange-traded fund (ETF) is similar to a mutual fund; both own baskets of investments, but an ETF trades on the stock market in the same way an individual common stock does. A trader can buy and sell the ETF any time the markets are open, and the commissions paid are at least as low as for a trade of common stock, sometimes lower. There are ETFs traded these days that track virtually everything and there are usually options traded that use the ETF for the underlying security. Choose carefully.

Exchange-traded funds differ from mutual funds in an important way. Mutual fund pricing is tallied up after the close; if you sell a mutual fund any time during the day you will get the closing price on that day. Depending on your broker's rules, you might be able to cancel a trade during the day, but you cannot buy and sell a mutual fund like a stock or an ETF and many mutual funds have stiff penalties for early exits. During the height of the crash I took a 2 percent early-out penalty for my Matthews China Mutual Fund rather than continue to watch it fall. To my knowledge, no one has figured out a way to trade options on mutual funds...yet.

Equivalent Option Trades

STRATEGY	EQUIVALENCE	STRATEGY
Naked call	Same as	Long stock + Long put
Naked put	Same as	Short stock + Long call
Long stock	Same as	Long call + Short put
Covered call	Same as	Sell naked put
Straddle	Same as	Short stock + Long calls or Long stock + Long puts
Bullish call spread Buy call lower strike Sell call higher strike	Same as	Bullish put spread Buy put lower strike Sell put higher strike
Bearish Call Spread Buy call higher strike Sell call lower strike	Same as	Bearish put spread Buy put higher strike Sell put lower strike

Chapter 6

US Treasury Bills

Safe-Deposit-Box America

The 1969 Western classic *Butch Cassidy and the Sundance Kid* was directed by George Roy Hill and written by William Goldman, who won the Academy Award for best original screenplay. The film stars Paul Newman as Butch Cassidy and Robert Redford as the Sundance Kid, and the plot takes Butch, Sundance, and Etta Place (played by the beautiful Katharine Ross) to Bolivia, where they are trying—unsuccessfully—to go straight. The two gunslingers take jobs guarding the mine payroll for the cranky old miner Percy Garris, played by the great character actor Strother Martin ("What we've got here is...failure to communicate"). On the way down the mountain to town, Butch and

Sundance are at the height of awareness, diligently scouring the trail for any possible ambush. As Percy sings to himself for company, Butch interrupts excitedly, "I think they're in the trees up ahead." Sundance, now also highly alert, responds, "In the bushes on the left." Then, with the fabulous chemistry the two great actors always showed when working together, they argue in the face of danger.

Butch: "I'm telling you they're in the trees up ahead."

Sundance: "You take the trees, I'll take the bushes."

Then, exasperated, the old miner interrupts.

Percy: "Will you two beginners cut it out?"

Butch: "Well, we're just trying to spot an ambush, Mr. Garris."

Percy: "Morons. I've got morons on my team. Nobody is going to rob us going down the mountain. We have got no *money* going down the mountain. When we have got the money, on the way back, then you can sweat."

***

In the old days, when governments went to war they would tax the hell out of their population to build up their war chest. Then the brilliant guys in the British Empire figured out—because they had the strongest banking system in the world—that they could borrow the money to fight their wars. Hey, they thought, this is great; if we don't win we won't have to pay back our debt. When America entered the First World War in 1917, they split the tab for the war between increased taxes and borrowing by selling Liberty Bonds. These bonds, over the years have evolved into the debt the US Treasury sells today.

In 1982 I was living alone in a four-hundred-square foot apartment on the water in Long Beach, California. The sounds of the ocean would gently lull me to sleep as I read a good book. I didn't buy my first television set for years because I thought it intellectually vacant— I got my first TV in 1989 after my artsy and beautiful live-in girlfriend booted me out for being a boring and elitist wannabe writer and full-time scientist. *I deserved it.* So one night as I was reading some obscure Victorian novel I got a call from a fire-breathing young stockbroker who was working late dialing cold calls. I don't know if he dialed my number randomly or if the beach address had impressed him—he couldn't have known that I was renting a converted lease office in the lobby next to the elevator shaft, the smallest apartment in a neighborhood of expensive beach condos. It did have a spectacular ocean view and only cost $200 per month.

The energetic broker was ecstatic when I didn't hang up on him; I was just as happy that a stockbroker had taken the time to call me at home. I was moving up in the world. He immediately began to tell me about the tremendous opportunity in Treasury bills. This is where I start to tune out these days. T-bills? I hadn't even wanted to get into a house because I thought I could do so much better in the stock market. Treasuries were the boring stuff of my dad's generation. But the broker was patient and explained that with double-digit interest rates the Treasuries were grossly underpriced. I should buy into his Treasury bond mutual fund and reap the harvest. I can't remember if I was intelligent enough to understand the opportunity or if he was just a great salesman, but I took him up on his offer and transferred my account into his control.

Sure enough, as time went on, the gigantic interest rates then Federal Reserve chairman Paul Volcker imposed to reign in stampeding inflation gradually worked their dark magic. And my share of the bond fund went up nicely—one of my first pleasant investments. Volcker's high-interest-rate solution was painful, but it worked a lot better than the Whip Inflation Now (WIN) buttons everyone in the Ford administration wore around during his short administration.

By the summer of 2012, when I finished the first draft of this book, it was just as Percy said to Butch and Sundance on the way down the mountain. There was no money in Treasuries; that is to say, there was way too much money in them, and we would be morons to buy them. The interest paid on the US ten-year Treasury bond had by this time dropped below 1.5 percent, *a two-hundred-year record low*. This means that the bond prices were at record highs.

By the end of 2012, the largest holder of US Treasury bonds was the People's Republic of China. Since the rise of the Chinese export economy, US paper has been one of the few places China can put the gigantic amounts of US dollars it has made selling us everything from the clothes we wear to the electronics we're so famous for inventing. Buying Treasuries also keeps the foreign-exchange rate for the renminbi low to support China's manufacturing and export system. But the obvious state of our economy and our tremendous national debt puts its investment at risk. After China's 2009 legislation session, the then Chinese premier said, "Of course we are concerned about the safety of our assets. To be honest, I'm a little bit worried...I would like to call on the United States to honor its words, stay a credible nation, and ensure the safety of Chinese assets."

The relationship between the rate paid and the price offered on government bonds is an inverse one; as the demand for the bonds drives the price up, the amount of interest needed to be paid to attract buyers goes down; as demand decreases, a higher interest rate is required to attract buyers. In the five years after the market break in October 2007, global investors flocked to the perceived safety of US government paper, driving the prices up and the rates down. The twenty-year and thirty-year bonds were paying astoundingly low rates of 2.2 percent and 2.6 percent, respectively. The Treasury bond auction in the second week of July 2012 was a tremendous success; global investors bought the ten-year Treasury with overwhelming demand, at a *negative real interest rate*. This is tantamount to investors *paying* the US government to hold their money for ten years. I wrote, "This is like getting a $100,000 home mortgage with a net ten-year payback of $99,000. Why does our government not borrow all they can and repair our aging infrastructure?" The rest of the world was begging to pay the United States to hold their money. It is what I call safe-deposit-box America: there is no interest paid on money held in a safe deposit box either. If our government was smart, which looks less and less likely with each congressional vote, we would issue a fifty-year Treasury bond and sell them until the market choked on them.

Sure, we'll hold your money for a fee. As Arnold Schwarzenegger's character in *Terminator* famously said, "No problemo!"

Terminator is the 1984 science fiction blockbuster that put Schwarzenegger's career on a rocket ship to the stars. Directed and cowritten by James Cameron, the movie starred Arnold, of course, as the robot terminator; Linda Hamilton as the mother of the hope of mankind, Sarah Connor; and Michael Biehn as Kyle Reese, the human who comes back in time to protect Sarah and unknowingly father the hope.

One market maven was quoted as saying that the government bond market was telling us that there would be little, if any, growth in America for the next thirty years. He scoffed at the notion and said that this could not be true. I hope not. The fear in early 2012 was that if the postcrash economy continued to mirror the one after the 1929 crash, we would be in for a long slow slog. The markets languished for twenty-five years after the Crash of 1929. By July 2012 my confidence that governments around the world would be able to use "borrow and spend" policies to avoid the worst case scenario of global deflation, of the sort that ravaged America during the Great Depression, was wavering.

I held tough to my hyperinflation big picture thesis as gold rolled over in late 2011 then really plummeted during the first half of 2012, and I lost hugely when the price of gold and every other hard commodity corrected. My inflation thesis looked evermore improbable as European governments, one by one, chose draconian austerity measures: less spending and higher taxes. These policies looked terrifyingly similar to the deflationary policies put in place in America in 1936, thereby initiating the horrible double dip in the economy that changed a severe recession into a seemingly endless depression.

Elsewhere in this book I make the case that buying Treasuries at record low interest rates is an inevitable loser. In 1982 I bought Treasuries when they were in the exact opposite condition: record high interest rates and record low prices. When interest rates came down, I made a big profit on the increase in the bond prices. I believe a break in the Treasury bond market is inevitable—in early 2012 I thought sometime in 2013, with the prices of the bonds going into free fall as interest rates skyrocket up. This time around, when this market breaks, anyone holding the bonds will take a huge hit.

By midsummer 2013, interest rates were on the rise and I played this move with call options on the TBT to short Treasuries and put options on the SPY to catch the downturn in the S&P caused by increasing interest rates. The trades were profitable but when the Fed decided not to taper their bond buying in September of 2013 they saved the market, but cost me money on the trade. (The TBT and the SPY are exchange traded funds, ETFs, designed to mimic the performance of specific market parameters. I used puts to bet against the SPY, which is long the S&P index, and calls to bet with the TBT, which is short Treasuries. See the Useful Stuff section for a list of ETFs and what they do.)

The big dogs, with their high-speed computers located in rooms next to the trading floors—allowing them to legally front-run the market—will be able to get out of Treasuries when they break, but all the little fleas will be the last ones to get out. Front-running is the illegal practice of buying or selling a stock or bond, using advance knowledge of a trade that will affect the price of the stock or bond when it is executed. It is illegal for a person to front-run the market, but for some reason when it is done by a computer, it's just smart business.

So far, in their fight against a deflation-based Armageddon, the US Federal Reserve Bank has managed to keep interest rates low. But political forces against these successful policies are gaining strength; you hear the vehemence of these forces on TV screaming that past Fed Chairman Ben Bernanke was un-American and has destroyed the American way of life. My personal signal that the Treasury market is primed for collapse will arrive when (or if) this faction of American political thinking gains control of the Fed. When the Treasury market breaks it will be very ugly for those holding the bonds, but the markets are a zero-sum game; those leaving Treasuries will need to go somewhere else. When all the investors who are crowded into Treasury investment stampede out, there will be only one other class of investment with the size and liquidity to take them—stocks.

Just as the market maven scoffed at the idea of an America without growth, I too am optimistic regarding America and growth over the next twenty-five or thirty years. America has always found a way to innovate and prove the doubters wrong. But it won't do us fleas much good if we lose everything in a Treasury-bond market collapse. So how do we trade this scenario? The stock market is the place, and since we don't know when the break will come we will need to have some income. That points to strong, America-based companies with good dividends and a history of actually paying them out and even increasing them over time. I have tried to load up a portfolio of these stocks a half a dozen times during the four years after the crash, and each time I have been too early or got chased out by my own emotions. In this book's companion volume, *The Stock Market Flea: Trading the Crash of 2008*, I include several iterations of my dividend portfolio, indicating some of my choices for dividend-paying stocks, but by the time you read this book they will be as stale as month-old options. You will need to do your own research to find the best dividend-paying stocks at the time you want to buy them.

So in 1982, with Treasury rates approaching 15 percent, it was a great investment to buy Treasuries, but in 2012, with rates that provided a negative real return, Treasuries were a fool's bet. Sure enough, by the middle of 2013 the tide had begun to turn and interest rates were pushing up in spite of the Fed's bond buying quantitative easing policies. Then Fed Chairman Bernanke postulated the need to reduce this bond buying, to "taper" the buying over time, and interest rates spiked. High dividend paying stocks, the utilities and telecoms that had done so well during quantitative easing, were hit hard. If my hyperinflation big-picture investment thesis does come to pass, the Federal Reserve will need to increase interest rates to gigantic levels to rein in the inflation I expect—and that will be the time to buy Treasuries. I know it sounds like I am talking out of both sides of my mouth—we need inflation now, inflation will be bad in the future—but that is exactly the place where we find ourselves today.

There is one new investment vehicle in the Treasury bond universe that may be a good long term investment should inflation become the problem—Treasury Inflation-Protected Securities.

Treasury Inflation-Protected Securities

Wikipedia defines US Treasury–issued paper as follows: "A United States Treasury security is a government debt issued by the United States Department of the Treasury through the Bureau of the Public Debt. Treasury securities are the debt-financing instruments of the United States federal government, and they are often referred to simply as Treasuries. There are four types of marketable treasury securities: Treasury bills, Treasury notes, Treasury bonds, and Treasury Inflation-Protected Securities (TIPS)."

There are many esoteric differences between the first three types of Treasury paper, but the big difference is the duration of the debt:

- Treasury bill—one year or less

- Treasury note—two to ten years

- Treasury bond—twenty to thirty years

The fourth type of debt the treasury issues are the TIPS, and they differ from the others in one important way: they have an inflation component. They are inflation-indexed bonds that are offered in five-, ten-, and thirty-year maturities. The TIPS have their principal indexed to the Consumer Price Index (CPI), so if the "price of stuff" goes up due to inflation, the amount the US Treasury will pay you back will also go up. Not a bad deal.

What's A Little Flea to Do?
So, with our money already losing value, Treasury bills selling at absurd prices, and inflation lurking just over the horizon, what can a flea do to protect his or her savings? There is always the trading of options, and you can bet I'll be there, but here are a few ideas for longer-term investment I'm considering for myself:

- A house with a thirty-year fixed-rate mortgage
- TIPS—treasury-backed inflation-protected bonds
- Gold, gold exchange-traded funds (ETFs), gold-mining stocks
- ETFs that bet on a strong Chinese currency
- ETFs that bet on the rise of new economies (China, Brazil, Indonesia),
- Mutual funds of proven managers for the strong emerging economies

If you are really, really brave—or dumb, depending on your viewpoint—and decide you want to short the Treasury market, there are some ETFs designed to do just that. Some of these ETFs are very dangerous: the ultrashort ETFs are twice (two times) leveraged and are compounded daily. So if the market goes against you, the losses are twice what the underlying Treasury moved. Worse, since the funds close everything out every day, you start the next day from scratch—but with less money. If the next day the Treasuries move back to where they started, moving down the same amount they went up the day before, you don't make your money back. On the first day a 10 percent loss on $100 brings you down to $90, but a 10 percent gain the next day will only bring you back to $99. Over time your investment can just get nibbled to death. I get around this dangerous accounting practice by buying very long dated call options on the ETF I want (like the TBT). The calls are less affected by the daily revaluing of the underlying ETF.

Exchange-Traded Funds That Short US Treasuries

Trading Symbol	Company	Type	Target
TBF	Proshares	Short	20-year Treasuries
TBX	Proshares	Short	7- to 10-year Treasuries
DTYS	IPath	Bear	10-year Treasuries
DTUS	IPath	Bear	2-year Treasuries
TBT	Proshares	Ultrashort	20-year Treasuries
PST	Proshares	Ultrashort	7- to 10-year Treasuries

The table above includes some of the ETFs out there that bet against the value of the Treasury market. They have different properties and bet against different durations of paper. It is far from a complete list. These leveraged ETFs are used by the big dogs to hedge other investments they are making, so a loss in these may mean big gains for them somewhere else. You really need to do your homework before using these instruments.

Chapter 7

Precious Metals

Fiat Currency, or Money Not Worth the Paper and Ink

In John Huston's 1948 movie *Treasure of the Sierra Madre*, starring Humphrey Bogart as Fred C. Dobbs, Tim Holt as Bob Curtin, and Walter Huston (John's dad) as Howard, it's all about the gold. The three improbable partners actually locate the gold deposit, mine it, and become instantly rich. But as usually happens in these things, greed raises its ugly head and Dobbs gets driven crazy by it. After surviving an attack of banditos where the iconic line "We don't need no stinking badges" is first heard, things go bad in a hurry. The gold is lost and Dobbs is killed.

Before all the mischief, even before they find the gold, Howard wisely says, "Ah, as long as there's no find, the noble brotherhood will last, but when the piles of gold begin to grow…that is when the trouble starts. I know what gold does to men's souls."

***

It has been said that gold is the ultimate currency. It has been used since ancient times in exchange for goods and services. The earliest reported use of gold as currency was when Lydian merchants produced the first gold coins in about 700 BCE, but the use of coins seems to have developed separately in China, India, and around the Aegean Sea at about the same time. In the world of numismatics, these coins were primitive, simply stamped lumps of the precious metal, but they heralded the new age of money. Before these first coins people just swapped items of value.

Much earlier, as far back as 12,000 BCE, there was a system of trade based on Anatolian obsidian, a critical raw material for toolmaking in the Stone Age, so the concept of an inherently valuable substance that was universally accepted for barter goes back to the very beginnings of civilization. Between about 9000 and 6000 BCE, cattle were used as an early type of money. The system of money that gradually developed was much more efficient; a few gold coins were a lot easier to carry than a cow or a basket of rocks.

During the Middle Ages, a form of European trade developed that was heavily supported through the use of credit. Commodities such as tin, wool, and sulfur, and finished products like wine, oil, and cloth, were provided to a buyer in exchange for a written promise to pay at some specific date in the future. These instruments were called *bills of exchange* and were one of the first forms of paper money. If the buyer was well known, the seller could redeem his bill of exchange for hard currency from a banker—for a price, of course.

In the twelfth century, the ever-creative English invented financial engineering when they came up with the tally stick. Cheaper to make and use than coins or paper money, tally sticks were pieces of wood that had notches cut into them to denote debts owed the Crown. It didn't take the Brits long to figure out that they could use the tally sticks to create money from thin air by cutting some new notches to represent *future* tax payments and use these future tallies as a form of payment for the current debts of the Crown. Clever, those English.

The so-called gold standard was a system for governments to exchange currencies between them. It never really meant that the paper currency was redeemable in gold. The British pound during the height of the empire was considered the strongest currency available and the closest equivalent to gold, but the Crown never had even a tiny fraction of the gold needed to redeem all of its paper money. Even during the Gold Rush days, between about 1850 and 1900, when America was belching up tons of the stuff, the US Treasury never backed more than 16 percent of the currency with gold reserves. That amount dropped to less than 1 percent by 1970.

Fiat money has been defined as "money that derives its value from government regulation of law: the initial value of the fiat money is established by government decree. The term fiat currency is also used when the fiat money is used as the main currency of the country. The term derives from the Latin fiat (let it be done, it shall be)."

In 1971, Richard Nixon, the sitting Republican president, instituted a series of economic measures, known as the Nixon Shock, which included unilaterally canceling the direct convertibility of the United States dollar into gold. This act caused the end of the Bretton Woods system of international financial exchange that had been in use since World War II. The Bretton Woods system was the first internationally agreed-upon system of monetary relations between independent nation-states. *Poof,* it was gone, along with a couple of hundred years of American financial strength.

By the end of the 1960s, due to an unfunded war in Vietnam and increased domestic spending, inflation was out of control. The proverbial crap hit the fan in 1970 when global arbitrage of the US dollar against our gold standard caused an international loss of faith in the US government's ability to cut the budget and trade deficits. *Now, does this sound familiar?*

Interestingly, Germany was the first to abandon the system, as it would have forced that country to devalue the deutsche mark in order to prop up the US dollar. In the months afterward, the German economy took off and the dollar went down almost 8 percent against the mark. *This is just getting too much like déjà vu all over again.*

But the US Treasury just kept on printing dollars, without the gold to back it up. Soon other countries, led by Switzerland and France, demanded the United States keep its promise and pay up in gold. The Chinese premier said pretty much the same thing in 2009 (see chapter 6). In August 1971, in a lame effort to control inflation and save the economy, Nixon imposed an impotent and idiotic wage and price freeze and closed the "gold window," thereby ending the convertibility of dollars into gold. And overnight America had a fiat currency.

By 1976, the year I graduated from college, global currencies were free-floating, the country was in a terrible recession that was accompanied by uncontrolled inflation (a condition that became known as "stagflation"), and there were no jobs to be found. I took my degree in biochemistry and became a bartender. Just before graduation, one of my buddies in the biochem department told me that his dad was buying gold, now that the price was unregulated. He was loading up on the stuff at $32 an ounce. Yeah, smart. His son, my buddy, is a smart guy too—he is teaching anesthesiology at the University of California–Irvine School of Medicine these days.

So if moving to a fiat currency is such a terrible idea, why did they do it? Any reasonable person might ask why the Nixon administration took us to a fiat currency when so many economists warned it of the eventual results.

The Vietnam War, like the current wars in Afghanistan and Iraq, was unfunded—that is, the money needed to fight the war was borrowed. And America needed to borrow *a lot* of money; war is very expensive. One .50-caliber bullet costs about $5. A single .50-caliber machine gun has a five-hundred-round-per-minute rate of fire. So the gun costs $2,500 per minute to operate. Scale this up for bombs and planes and you quickly get into real money. With the debt incurred to fight the Vietnam War exceeding $200 billion ($11.25 trillion in 2011 dollars); the US government realized it could never pay back the debt. But wait a minute! If it instituted highly inflationary policies it could pay the debt back in dollars worth much less than when it borrowed them. Remember the 17 percent inflation during the late 1970s?

But before it could inflate the currency, it needed first to get off the gold standard. This was quite an underhanded move on the bond investors who lent the government the money. If you were holding government bonds during the next ten years, you got killed as interest rates went from 3 to 17 percent because, as discussed in chapter 6, the price of the bond goes down rapidly as the interest rate goes up.

The same thing is happening now. Why pay back a debt at a hundred cents on the dollar when it is within your power to pay it back at fifty or twenty-five or ten cents on the dollar? This is great for the government but terrible for the saver. The value of the dollars you have in your savings account were debased by about 13 percent during 2011 and it continues to decline. Only the global economic crisis, which has the world teetering on the brink of global deflation—the worst-case demon of the 1930s—has kept this inflation in check...so far.

Former vice president Dick Cheney famously said, "Ronald Reagan proved that deficits don't matter." He could not have been more mistaken.

What is wrong with these guys?

During the night of August 11, 2011, the Chicago Mercantile Exchange (CME) increased margin requirements for speculators who buy gold on the cuff. This is, in real-people terms, similar to the down payment on a mortgage, only they don't have to pay it; they just need to have it. This was only the first of many increases in the margin requirements that were an unabashed effort to control the increase in the price of gold. The next day the short-term trend in gold was broken. Although I'm still a believer that gold will increase in the long term, short-term selling pressure, especially in the SPDR Gold Shares ETF (the GLD) caused me to adjust my gold and silver positions.

The CME's decision to increase the margin requirements on speculators buying gold futures broke the uptrend in gold. This destroyed the value of a position I had in GLD calls that had been working very well for me until their move. The increase in margin requirements was the ringing of the bell signaling the short-term top in gold. As a trader, I had to exit my position in the metal when repeated increases in the new margin requirements finally broke the short-term uptrend. The price of gold dropped over $200 per ounce by mid-2012 and continued to drift lower until forming a bottom on June 28, 2013, when it closed below $1,200 per ounce. After a short recovery it retested these lows in December 2013.

I still think the huge global debt will force governments to inflate away the principal of that debt and the demand for gold will overwhelm their efforts to slow down speculation in the precious metal, the only true currency. But I'm afraid this crisis looks more like the stagflation of the 1970s than the rebound after the 1987 and 2008 crashes. Once inflation really takes hold, the Federal Reserve will need to increase interest rates to regain control, just like Paul Volcker did in the early 1980s. I'm waiting to put every cent into US Treasuries once the interest rate on the thirty-year bond reaches, say, 15 or 18 percent.

> **Lesson:** *When the CME increases the margin requirements on gold futures, listen to the bell ringing in the top of the market. The long-term uptrend may hold, but don't fight city hall—get out and watch from the sidelines.*

In November 2009 I watched as the usual obnoxious talking heads were screaming at one another on CNBC—screaming and not listening. One side of the argument was a rabid call for inflation, and the other side was a wild-eyed forecast of deflation. This was very interesting to me, as several of my partners had asked me where we were and where we were going in the future. What should they do? Where should they invest? Are we moving into an inflationary period, as most prognosticators are saying, or are we going to have a repeat of 1930s deflation? Which way and how do they play it?

My standard answer when answering this question was, "I am not smart enough to know, but it doesn't matter. Not if you stay nimble as a flea and trade the market."

Here are two excellent books that I recommend everyone read: *Conquer the Crash* by Robert R. Prechter Jr. (2002) and *The Collapse of the Dollar* by James Turk and John Rubino (2004). Both books have been rereleased recently with updates.

The first book, *Conquer*, is based on the Elliott Wave Theory, which says the economy and the market behave as they do because of the mood of the masses—are you optimistic or pessimistic?—and can be quantified with fractal mathematics. In short, the big picture has the same shape as the micropicture. Without getting into the details, Prechter says the markets topped in 2000, we are in the midst of a disaster, and the bull market we have had since March 2009 is ready to turn back down. Prechter predicts a deflationary depression that will dwarf the Great Depression of the 1930s. He uses *the fiat monetary system, the huge debts of the nation and the people, and predictable, if disastrous, governmental policy*, to validate his conclusion. But it is really the shape of the stock market charts that convinces him.

In the second book, *Collapse*, Turk and Rubino use historical examples of monetary collapse from ancient Rome through prerevolutionary France and the Weimar Republic of Germany between the World Wars and finish with the currency crisis of 1998 that destroyed the currency and economy of Argentina. They don't say it, but remember how all these ended: the sack of Rome, the Napoleonic Wars, World War II, and the Falkland Islands war, respectively. Turk and Rubino predict hyperinflation as the inevitable result of...*the fiat monetary system, the huge debts of the nation and the people, and predictable, if disastrous, governmental policy.*

If you want to hear more about the fiat monetary system ("money for nothing and chicks for free") you might want to visit the Internet. Just type "fiat money" into your search engine and stand back, although you should be prepared for a fringe view of the whole thing.

Here is the punch line: they both get to the same place eventually—Prechter, who says deflation is inevitable, and Turk and Rubino, who predict hyperinflation; both recommend gold as the only safe investment. But they go further than a simple call to buy gold, because in 1932 the US government outlawed the possession of gold. This happened historically, in very similar ways, in Rome, France, Germany, and Argentina too. The governments eventually thus own all the value. Prechter says that in his doomsday postcollapse world, you won't need to worry about roving packs of thugs, like in *Mad Max*, but you will need to worry about governmental control and seizure—like in *Atlas Shrugged*.

Mad Max is the 1979 Australian action film that takes the repressive, controlling state for a drive out on the highway. Directed by George Miller and starring Mel Gibson, the movie has become a cult classic. *Atlas Shrugged* is the movie I use to start chapter 11.

Although the authors of each book seem to have personal axes to grind and may benefit financially from their recommendations, they both recommend a new kind of money that is based on gold held in safe places like Switzerland, but existing only in the uncontrolled ether of the Internet: "Goldmoney." It works like an electronic checkbook. If you have to run across borders, it is easier to carry than gold bars. You can check this out at http://www.goldmoney.com.

Of course, there is a third possibility. This less spectacular possibility is that the economy will recover as it did after other crashes in 2003, 1987, 1983, 1975, 1946, 1932, 1865, 1838, 1790, and so on. You get the idea. Still, I wonder if we are going to have another move down—the dreaded W-shaped recovery. At the time of this printing, I'm still overweighted in cash. But maybe I should get some of this new goldmoney stuff.

When I was researching the relationship between gold and greed—it seems a pretty easy relationship—I was blasted with the Internet claims about the Union Bank of New York scandal. The Union Bank of New York was a prominent investment bank that was seized during World War II under the Trading with the Enemy Act (1917). The bank was operated as a clearinghouse for the American assets and enterprises held by German steel magnate Fritz Thyssen and his family. It was claimed initially that the bankers were hiding gold for their Nazi customers, although these claims were almost universally disproved. After exhaustive investigation, however, it was found that the Thyssens did control the bank, and in 1942 the bank was seized. After the seizure the bank's assets were held for the duration of the war and then released afterward. The primary reason the episode is remembered today at all is when it is used by the radical Left as a political tool to besmirch the Bush family; George W. Bush's grandfather, Prescott Bush, was a director and vice president of Union Bank of New York during the war. I find it very improbable that the father of our first President Bush would have been actively aiding the enemy with his son flying dangerous missions and getting shot down over the Pacific. The Anti-Defamation League and others who investigated Prescott Bush came to the conclusion that his involvement with the scandal was purely commercial. In 2003, the Anti-Defamation League said: "Rumors about the alleged Nazi 'ties' of the late Prescott Bush...have circulated widely through the Internet in recent years. These charges are untenable and politically motivated. Despite some early financial dealings between Prescott Bush and a Nazi industrialist named Fritz Thyssen, Prescott Bush was neither a Nazi nor a Nazi sympathizer."

I find it much more interesting that in these days of American political royal families—like the Kennedys, the Clintons, and the Bushes (even the Libertarians who are so adamantly against such inherited power have their own nascent royalty in Ron and Rand Paul) — that "W" and Jeb have affected the facade of good old boys from Texas when for generations the Bush family has been one of old Northeastern money, have attended Yale and become masters of banking, industry, and East Coast politics.

On March 6, 2009, the generational bottom, I told my newsletter readers that I was buying gold and silver. On February 14, 2011, I wrote, "Today the

Dow-Gold Ratio—the number of ounces of gold required to buy the Dow 30 Stocks—was at a seventeen-year low of 7.03." There was an increase in the relative value of gold of 27.5 percent after my newsletter call.

In retrospect, looking back with the perfect perspective of the historian, August 2011 would have been a great time to take profits and sell gold while December of 2013 may have been a great time to get back in. I took my medicine on my gold (GLD) position but I chose to hang on to my silver (SLV) investment.

There are many ways to trade gold or the other precious metals such as silver and platinum. There seem to be as many opinions about the best method of holding gold as there are experts espousing those opinions. Each method has positives and negatives associated with it. Gold metal can be purchased as:

- Bullion, in weights ranging from one grain (0.0022857 ounces) to one kilogram (35.2739 ounces) or even larger for banks and reserves.

- Coins with many weights and purities minted in many countries.

- Jewelry made from the metal.

- Exchange-traded funds (ETFs) that hold the metal in reserves.

- Gold mining stocks.

Having the actual metals in one's possession is favored by those who believe the global economy is going to fold, that the only money that will have value in the postapocalypse world will be gold and silver. Holding gold or silver bullion requires the owner to make adequate arrangements to protect the metal while still maintaining a ready method of getting to it. Bullion can be stored in a bank safe deposit box, but if the banks are closed it might as well be on the moon. It can be buried in the backyard, but a neighbor's dog might locate the spot while hunting for bones. In the mattress might prove to be too uncomfortable for a sound night's sleep. If the purpose of the purchase is to have precious metal after the decline of civilization, a two-pound bar of gold might be just a little hard to use, and it might paint a giant target on the owner's back.

Owning gold coins presents the same dilemma as bullion for storage and access, but it does have the advantage of being a little easier to exchange in the dark times after the rule of law has become a thing of the past. Still, brandishing a chest of gold coins might bring the same unwanted attention as it brought to the wagon train of settlers in the movie *Silverado* (1985). Produced and directed by Lawrence Kasdan, *Silverado* has an entertaining story—the screenplay was also a product of Kasdan's ample creativity—and an ensemble cast that is impossible not to love: Kevin Kline, Scott Glenn, Danny Glover, Kevin Costner, John Cleese, and Brian Dennehy, to name some of the most recognizable. Once the wagon-train settlers show their chest of gold coins, every outlaw in the territory follows them out on the trail. It takes the best effort of the good guys, Kline and the rest, to recover the stolen gold and see the settlers to the end of the trail.

Gold jewelry might be just the thing for someone who is preparing for the end-time. In the 1976 British science fiction movie *The Man Who Fell to Earth*, rock star David Bowie plays an alien who becomes trapped on earth. Directed by Nicolas Roeg, the film also stars Candy Clark and Rip Torn. When the alien arrives on our unfamiliar planet, he brings with him a string of gold wedding rings he uses to purchase whatever he needs without drawing attention to himself. Each time he barters away the ring on his finger he simply takes another one from his hidden store and puts it on. The bad guys never suspect he has a fortune in gold stashed just out of sight.

When an investor buys the physical metals, he or she should be very sure of the source. There have been many scams to cheat investors of their investment dollars. These schemes range from not delivering the metal at all, to selling counterfeit bullion and coins, to sophisticated ways to take a little of the float by not delivering the metal in a timely fashion. There will always be scoundrels hovering around the legitimate precious-metals marketplace; this is clearly a case where "buyer beware" holds true.

If, on the other hand, a trader believes as I do that the economic world will do as it has always done and recover over time, there are many alternative methods for investing in precious metals other than holding the physical bullion. My favorites are ETFs that hold the precious metals in secure reserves and precious-metal mining stocks.

The ETFs can be bought and sold easily on the open market like stocks. When you buy the ETF you buy a portion of the stored metal. There are many precious-metal ETFs, but some of the most common, and therefore those with the most liquid markets, are the SPDR Gold Shares ETF (the GLD), which represents one-tenth of an ounce of gold; the iShares Silver ETF (the SLV), which represents an ounce of silver; the iShares Gold ETF (the IAU), which represents one-hundredth of an ounce of gold. These ETFs are backed by the physical gold and silver. There are many such ETFs (SGOL, USV, SIVR, etc.), so some homework is in order before they are purchased. There are also ETFs for the gold-mining stocks such as the GDX and the GDXJ.

Precious-metal mining stocks can be a good way to invest in the underlying metals; they can also be the worst. Mining stocks have leverage, because the profits of a company that produces the metal increase at a faster rate than the cost of the metal. Some companies pay small dividends, and company-specific information can be used to find the best of breed within the group of companies. An ETF will usually bag up the good with the bad. The downside of the mining stocks is that, like any common stock, they are subject to the winds of the market, poor corporate governance, and acts of God. My AEM stock tanked when a mine the company owned was flooded. The price of gold and the GLD didn't budge, but the AEM stock got hammered. There are also the precious-metal penny stocks that are always being pumped by the investors in the companies. These penny stocks are usually not for me. Yes, a few will have spectacular returns when the companies hit it big, but most will simply go broke. The challenge is guessing which ones are which.

Chapter 8

Real Estate

Leverage, or Playing by the Big Dogs' Rules

In the hilarious 1986 comedy *The Money Pit*, directed by Richard Benjamin and produced by Steven Spielberg, Tom Hanks (Walter) and Shelley Long (Anna) star as a New York City couple who buy a fixer-upper in the country. The house is a disaster, a contractor's dream come true, with every repair, large and small, estimated to be completed in two weeks, and every job going over budget. When Anna wonders why the house is such a deal, Walter says, "This is the short line in Motor Vehicles...You go to Motor Vehicles...and you get on this line that reaches to Spain, and right next to it is this little short line with only two guys on it, but you don't get on that line, 'cause you think something must be wrong with it—otherwise everyone else would be on it—so you waste three hours!" Then Anna replies, "I got on the short line once. It was for farm vehicles."

***

When I was offered a job in Hawaii in 1991, the company sent me for a week of vacation to see if I liked it there. I spent the entire week house hunting and was ready to make an offer on a place as I got back on the plane for the mainland—before I'd accepted the job.

My agent in Hawaii, Jana Hunt, was a real trouper and showed me place after place that I didn't like. Finally, out of desperation she took me out leeward, passed Waipahu. This was before the city of Kapolei was built and way before Disney bought into the Ihilani Resort. The area was the real Hawaii, out on the road the tourist guides recommended you shouldn't take—in a neighborhood, Honokai Hale, where the people who worked in the Waikiki hotels lived. I would be the only Haole in the neighborhood for years. The house was large for Hawaii, a rabbit warren of rooms that had been rented to make ends meet; upstairs was a huge living room, a bath, and three bedrooms, and there was a second floor cut into the hillside below. When we viewed the house I immediately fell in love with the spectacular 220-degree view over the Ko O'lina Golf Club and on to the blue Pacific Ocean.

But the place was a mess, not just because of the filth inside and out, the greasy Jeep parts in the front yard, and carpets so grimy they caused Jana to throw Hawaiian tradition to the wind and refuse to remove her shoes before entering. The place was built out of sticks and rocks—two-by-two framing and a moss rock foundation. When we got to the dizzying, boat-like, spiral staircase to the floor below, I couldn't go down; the stench of cat urine billowing up from the darkness was just too sickening. I told Jana to go down and tell me what she could see. Always the professional, she took a huge breath and spiraled downward. When she came back up, her face contorted from the smell, she said, "There is another big living room down there and a huge bathroom, and I found two more bedrooms."

"This is it," I said.

Jana's eyes grew wide, and I thought she was going to tell me I was nuts. But she worked on the deal as I moved out of my Naples Island place back in Long Beach, California, sending me piles of photos and forwarding faxes she had been exchanging with the absentee landlord in Japan. He wanted almost a half million dollars for the place and I offered half that amount. Jana said he would probably back out of the deal because my offer was a huge insult and he would lose face if he accepted it. But he was desperate—my kind of seller—having become overextended when the Japanese real estate bubble popped between 1989 and 1991. I told Jana that no one had a gun to his head; he could go on losing money by owning it, or he could sell it to me.

He sold, and I spent the next six years working on the place, doing much of the work myself but knowing when I needed help, and how much that help should reasonably cost. It was a real challenge, as it was before the big, mainland-based building supply stores like Home Depot had arrived. I bought a shovel in one small hardware store—its sale price was similar to what I was used to paying in California—but the pick that went with it was ten times the mainland cost. But the pick was on sale in another tiny hardware store and I drove across the island to buy it. Until Home Depot moved in at the mainland-style shopping center built in the new city of Kapolei, that was how I bought all my materials, in the true Hawaiian fashion: going anywhere for a bargain or a discount. When I left Hawaii for Asia the house was beautiful, and I hated leaving it.

This is really not a real estate book. I want to concentrate on the stock and options markets here. There is little doubt, however, that real estate is the single most important part of a long-term investment plan. There is no other investment in America that has as much governmental protection and support, no other investment with as many tax advantages. I can hear the arguments already, but let's keep it simple for now. There is no other investment, other than the options market, perhaps, with as much inherent leverage. I will discuss leverage in more detail later on. And most important, there is no other investment you and your family can sleep in. Staying in out of the rain is a critical factor in successful, long-term investing.

Let me say it again: real estate is the single most important part of a long term investment plan. The younger you are, the more important it is to you. It is even more important now, after the worst real estate devaluation since the 1929 crash. The 1929 crash had its underpinnings in a real estate bubble juiced by artificially low interest rates—just like today.

I bought my first stock when I was about twenty-four years old. I bought my first bonds and options when I was about twenty-seven years old. I bought my first real estate when I was about thirty-two years old. This is totally upside down—I was sleeping upside down like a bat. When I've got something totally wrong I'm not a bull or a bear, or even a flea; I'm a bat. Oh, the power of hindsight. My only excuse is that I have always been a wanderer at heart and when I was in my twenties I thought real estate would tie me down. You can't take it with you, you know. My reasoning looks pretty dumb from this vantage point.

In 2003 I sold the second piece of real estate I ever purchased, a beach condo on Naples Island in Long Beach, California. The first property I bought was with a girlfriend who wound up with it in the end. I lived in the Naples place about a year and a half before I was transferred to Hawaii. *It's tough work, but someone has to do it.* The renter who moved into it when I left town was very reluctant to sign a one-year lease, but I insisted since I would be so far away. She was still renting the property when I sold it fourteen years later—bound only by the original lease that had reverted to a month-to-month after the first year. Fourteen years of tax advantages including all the maintenance costs, one trip back to the mainland a year to check up on the property, and the all-important mortgage interest deduction. I also enjoyed a gradual increase in the appraised value of the property, a good renter who paid the mortgage every month and, notably, the building of a loan payment history that lenders really liked. This pleasant deal ended in a double based on my buy price when I sold the property, but the sale price was about ten times the amount I had put down to buy the property fourteen years earlier.

Here is a simple example of leverage: You want to buy a house—with a water view, of course. The purchase price is $250,000. *Yeah, right, maybe in Panama—but this is just an example.* You get a loan at, say, 6 percent and 20 percent down—good-bye and good riddance to 0 percent down, interest-only loans. Let's assume you are in the 25 percent tax bracket and for this example we'll make the property tax a push. The amount you get in interest for your savings is 3 percent. *I know—where can you get that rate?* In 2008 it was a crime to accept anything this low; but by 2012 rates this high were history. Just bear with me for the sake of the example. Here is how the numbers would work out if you kept the house for five years and it went up 30 percent in value. From a post-crash vantage point this seems a little ridiculous, but it has happened again and again, and I have told my readers, "It could be happening again right now."

Comparing Cash versus Borrowing to Buy Real Estate

	CASH PURCHASE	BORROWED MONEY
Cash down	−$250,000	−$50,000
Property tax	Same either way	Same either way
Monthly mortgage payment	$0	−$1500
Differential savings interest	$0	+$500
Differential tax savings	$0	+$300
Net monthly outlay	$0	−$700
Total investment in 5 years	−$250,000	−$92,000
Sale price	+$325,000	+$325,000
Profit	+$75,000	+$233,000
Percent gain per year	6 percent	18.6 percent

Take a look at the table above and the comparison of using cash to buy real estate versus using a mortgage. The real estate goes up the same amount either way, but the mortgaged property generates 19 percent profit in five years versus 6 percent profit if the property was purchased with cash. This is leverage.

> **Lesson:** *Never buy real estate with cash if you can borrow the money. There are a lot of reasons I think this and I get arguments about it all the time. The biggest reason is leverage. (Leverage is important in real estate, but it is critical in options trading.)*

Looks very good in that example, three times the leverage, but it doesn't always work. Take the recent swoon in housing. Many people maximized their leverage to speculate in the housing boom of the late 1990s and early 2000s; but now, with the drop in property values and the disappearance of credit, they find themselves losing money at the same rate they had sought to make it. Even the experts took a hit.

Take Bear Stearns as a painful example. The company was leveraged up somewhere around thirty or forty times. When the credit crisis hit, it couldn't cover its obligations to its creditors and went belly-up overnight. If the government had not stepped in to save the markets, we would all have felt the pain—that is, more than we are feeling it now. But if home buyers' first goal is to have a roof over their heads, I think patience will bring them back to even, and more, in time. Several properties I bought in the late 1980s and early 1990s got upside down when the recession brought on by the savings and loan debacle drove real estate values down. It took time—almost a decade—but eventually the values returned. Lee Viera, a Southern California loan broker I have worked with for years, once told me that the real estate market goes up and it goes down, but the highs and lows are always higher than before. I believe him, even though the price curve does not prove him to be correct in the short term.

I returned from living and working in Asia as an American expatri-ate just before the turn of the millennium. I had been living outside of North America for almost ten years when my company got bought out by a bigger fish and I was eventually repatriated to San Francisco. The good news was that I had been a middle manager for Betz Laboratories for many years, and since they had been a fair and prosperous company, I had a drawer full of stock options. The top managers at Betz had nego-tiated a great price for the debt-loaded company—double what it was trading for on the open market—so everyone who had options, espe-cially old ones with very low strikes, made out like thieves. The options were automatically exercised with the closing of the deal.

The option profits I received from the buyout in the late nineties, however, would not compensate me for taking the expatriate package that moved me to Asia. I had tried to limit the time I would commit to the expatriate assignment, but my new boss had required I sign on for at least three years. The three-year agreement forced me to sell my house in Hawaii at the bottom of the real estate market. Fortunately for me, the expat deal included a home buyout option, and I took it. The Hawaii house did not turn out to be the big winner I had expected, but Betz bought the house from me for everything I had invested in it—the buy price and the cost of all my upgrades—but not the time, effort, and sweat I had expended doing the work. It was a good way out of a prop-erty during a time when nothing was selling on my part of the island.

I had bought way out leeward in Oahu and the location wasn't yet one where you could be an absentee landlord, as suggested by the con-dition in which Jana and I had found the place originally. My plan was based on my belief that the area would soon be developed and the prop-erty values in the area would all rise as a result, but the crash of the real estate market in Japan in the early 1990s rippled through to Hawaii as if our islands were part of Japan. Japanese buyers had been buoying the Hawaiian real estate market for years, so Hawaii real estate crashed too. In 2011 Disney moved into the neighborhood with the Aulani Resort and my expectations were realized, twenty years too late. Well, that's just what we call Hawaii time.

When Betz was taken over by Hercules, however, the new company reneged on my expatriate contract and I found myself not repatriated back to my home in Hawaii but to San Francisco. By this time my bosses at the Betz headquarters were all hiding under their desks, trying not to be noticed. They told me a move back to Hawaii might raise eyebrows with the new owners. *Huh? It's not a vacation, it's where I live.*

When I got back to the United States, I was stunned by both the price of real estate and the upward acceleration of these prices. I decided that the real estate market was a bubble and chose to rent. I rented for a year in the Bay Area and then another year in Los Angeles, and every month, as I wrote my rent check, I watched as home prices continued to go up. I wondered how long it could last.

I was also flabbergasted by the rolling blackouts of a failed power system when I got back to America. It reminded me of Manila, where the power system was so unreliable that every restaurant had a big diesel generator on the sidewalk outside. At the time I thought it ridiculous. How could any country in the modern industrial world be so backward? I had started out working for Southern California Edison (SCE), where the inside joke had been that the customers on the outside didn't know what it took to create the electricity; "it's just always there when they flip the switch." While I had been gone, deregulation had destroyed the integrity of the electrical power system and Enron had gamed the system of Wild West banditry. SCE had sold all its power plants except the one big nuke and had shifted its concentration to its distribution system. It seemed to me that America was in retrograde motion. I had heard about deregulation, but it only became real when I lived it. My old friends who had thought their jobs at SCE were unassailable were now working in the real world—if they were lucky enough to be working at all.

It reminded me of what had happened in China while I was there. The workers in the old Mao-era factories, which were the pinnacle of inefficiency, had also believed their jobs secure—so secure that the jobs were called their "iron rice bowl." In the old China your job was your rice bowl; an iron rice bowl was a government-owned-factory job that was as unbreakable as iron. While I was working there, the government closed the inefficient factories without warning and told the workers they would need to find new jobs. Many of these workers became taxi drivers, and some of the *lucky* ones saved and begged and borrowed from their families to buy a taxi. Then a couple of years later the government passed a law, because of the overwhelming air pollution, that proclaimed that all taxis must be newer-model cars. The poor guys with taxis older than the cutoff date were out of luck. This is the power of the Chinese economic system. The government can do whatever it likes, whenever it likes; the people are helpless. The Chinese are becoming more like us and we are becoming more like them; the two systems are converging into corporatism.

I had sold my big house in Hawaii before moving to Asia, but I still had the nice little place on Naples Island in Long Beach, California. The Naples place had been rented by the same woman, a real estate loan broker, for over a decade, so I didn't want to displace her. When I got back to the Los Angeles area I moved farther north on the coast to the South Bay. I rented an apartment right on the water in Manhattan Beach, and began to shop for a new real estate investment property. Finally, in 2002 I bought a duplex in Manhattan Beach—a run-down place with a view of the Pacific Ocean and the Manhattan Beach Pier.

It was everything I look for in an investment property: it had a view of the water, it was run-down but fixable—I'm handy and do a lot of the work myself, it was the ugliest house in a great neighborhood, and the seller was desperate—going bankrupt and an absentee landlord. I couldn't even get in to view the unit I would later live in while I did the renovations because the ten or fifteen surfers inhabiting the place wouldn't let the real estate agents in for show-ings. When I did finally get inside, the unit was a mess: the hardwood floors were so water damaged I was afraid I would fall through, the walls were covered with juvenile murals of surfing and the sea, the kitchen was indescribably filthy and damaged and—worst of all— several of the surfers had been living, untidily, in the tiny attic crawl space—the floor up there was spotted with roaches; and I don't mean the kind with legs.

It was perfect and I told my agent so. She had shown me dozens of beautiful houses I had turned down, and when I told her that this was the one, I thought she would faint.

By the time I was finished renovating this gem the monthly rents were above $3,000 per month for each unit, double what I was paying on the newly refinanced, zero-down, interest-only, ten-year loan— one of the poisonous ones that ultimately brought down the system. I could live in one unit and pay for the entire duplex with the income from the other. I loved the place and Manhattan Beach and my short commute to the airport (LAX); I had found and created my dream house. And if I ever needed more room, I could combine the two units into one spectacular four-bedroom, three-bath beach house. I never wanted to leave.

But then, suddenly, it was 2006, and the bubble I had been wor-rying about for years seemed frothier than ever. So in August 2006, I sold my dream house, put most of my stuff into storage, and once again became a renter. I had already sold the beach condo on Naples Island, so the Manhattan Beach duplex was the last piece of real estate I owned. I got a double on the Naples place and almost a triple on the Manhattan Beach place. While it took barely four years for the Manhattan Beach property to triple, the Long Beach condo had taken fourteen years to double, after being upside down for years after the savings and loan crisis of 1986–91. August 2006 would turn out to be the exact peak of the real estate bubble. I had learned my lesson and got out while the getting was good.

Lesson: *If you can see water from a property (ocean, lake, river, or harbor), you can't lose. There is only so much property with water views and people will pay a premium for it. Even if the market turns down, it will come back to you eventually.*

Real Estate Investment Trusts

Real estate investment trusts, or REITs, are companies that specialize in real estate and real estate–related investments. Some own and manage real estate properties and others specialize in the mortgages, including the mortgage-backed securities (MBSs) that were so critical to the meteoric rise in real estate values and then the deafening crash of the real estate and stock markets in 2008. But don't let that scare you off; there are plenty of great MBSs out there, and some of these guys make a ton of money with them. After all, I paid back *my* toxic loan and so did many, many others. REITs are great for investors because they are required to pay out a least 90 percent of total taxable income to the owners to get the tax advantages of a REIT. This is similar to the way limited master partnerships work in the oil and energy world. I have listed some of the biggest and most successful REITs in the "Useful Stuff" section at the end of the book.

Chapter 9

Oil and Energy

The American Industry, or How Long Will We Get Screwed?

In the classic 1956 movie *Giant*, directed by George Stevens and starring Elizabeth Taylor and James Dean, Elizabeth's character Leslie Benedict is the beautiful wife of a big-money rancher, Jordan "Bick" Benedict, played by Rock Hudson. James Dean is the self-made millionaire Jett Rink who destroys his life in the lonely pursuit of money. Before young Jett's oil well comes in, Leslie tells him, "Money isn't everything..." Jett replies, "Not when you've got it."

***

I worked my entire adult life in the energy industry, and it is one of the things I have very strong feelings about. Since you have read this far in this book, you know by now that I can be very opinionated about a lot of things I don't know nearly as much about. It is my opinion that the problem with the American oil economy is not too little oil; the problem is too little leadership—both political and corporate. Let me try to explain.

Energy is the lifeblood of America. Everything Americans do in their everyday lives, everything they consume, everything they aspire to be or have, is dependent on energy. America consumes over half of the world's oil each day. The problem, as I see it, is that over the years, energy has become synonymous with oil. America invented the oil industry. Before oil, Americans were lighting their homes with whale oil (no kidding). Then the Yankee ingenuity that has made us great came into play in a remote part of western Pennsylvania. There, the oil was so close to the ground's surface that it would seep up into little pools that had little economic use and messed up the farmland.

Then the ever-imaginative Americans figured out that if they put the oil into a still they could isolate the part that was a good replacement for the whale oil, the stuff we now call kerosene. This breakthrough rang the bell that signaled the end of whale oil–fueled lamps. I'm sure if the whales had understood the magnitude of the discovery, they would have breathed a blowhole sigh of relief.

While distilling the crude oil to make kerosene for their lamps, the early refiners produced a pesky, lighter fraction for which they had no use. They burned this inconvenient lighter part to get rid of it—this is the product we now call gasoline.

Later, big cities were lighted first with natural gas and then by electricity, but the distillation of oil was here to stay. When another historic innovation, the automobile, came along, cheap, abundant fuel made the hitherto interesting, if ineffectual, contraption the wave of the future. This was a good thing for America; after all, America would be the world's largest producer of oil—the title Saudi Arabia holds now—for decades to come. Thus America's oil-based economy was born. It just made good sense at the time.

Some of the stories I've heard oil business old-timers tell are a lot of fun. One is the tale of how oil came to be measured the way it is today. Oil is measured in forty-two-gallon barrels now and hardly anyone can remember why. The old-timer story is that when they were just getting started, they would haul the oil from the well head to the still site over undeveloped country roads. They would put fifty-five-gallon drums of oil into the backs of the horse-drawn wagons and bump over the poor Pennsylvania roads, spilling the oil out from the uncovered drums as they traveled. This angered the buyers at the end of the road who claimed they were not getting full drums for their money. To clear up their differences, the producers and the buyers agreed to assign each of the drums a volume of forty-two gallons when it arrived. And this is the size of a barrel of oil to this day.

The world economy, and especially the American economy, took off based on cheap fuel and the internal combustion engine. But the handwriting has always been on the wall. The geopolitical distribution of the oil has been a burning fuse for decades. The unequal distribution of this critical military commodity has caused the world a lot of trouble. During World War II, the Germans invaded the Caucasus and the Japanese invaded the Dutch East Indies to get more of it (there were also other, more sinister reasons, of course). Some people think that when our government says America has strategic interests in the Middle East the meaning is we need Middle Eastern oil.

The oil-based economy was good for America when we were the world's largest producer of oil, but it doesn't seem to make much sense now. Our leaders, political and corporate, have done little to guide us into the next phase of energy development. The conspiracy theorist will provide you with ample reasons for this lack of leadership; I will not venture into it. My point is we don't need to stay on the oil-based economy and our leaders have failed us over the last thirty years.

This is especially true now that innovations have made us the Saudi Arabia of natural gas. Yes, there are concerns regarding the "fracking" process, but remember that they have been "shooting" oil wells in western Pennsylvania for over a hundred years without significant problems. Not counting the guys who got blown up doing it.

I was in college during the oil embargo of 1973, spending my share of time in the long gasoline lines and worrying if I would be able to find the gas to get home for Christmas. It seemed to me then that we needed to do something about our dependence on foreign oil; it was a huge problem, and many of our political leaders promised to do something about it, but over the next few years nothing really changed. Sometimes we had gas and sometimes we didn't.

The gas lines were back with a vengeance by 1979 and our leaders kept on promising solutions. I was tending bar on Bourbon Street in New Orleans at the time, and the river and the port were crowded with oil tankers. Gas was breaking through the half-dollar barrier and one of my customers joked without mirth, "I bet there is a whole lot of forty-cent gas on those tankers."

But quietly, almost imperceptibly, there was a change occurring. Again, American ingenuity and the American free market system were slowly making a course correction in our energy-based economy. Yes, capitalism is a good thing, within certain humanistic boundaries.

In 1980 I was a young chemist in a power plant complex in the Mojave Desert of Southern California. In this complex, Southern California Edison (SCE) was developing new technologies to deal with the high cost and poor availability of imported oil. The same innovation was happening across the country, even across the world, but I will use the SCE story as an example. At this power plant site SCE built the first modern solar thermal power plant—Solar One. Yes, it was a demonstration plant that didn't turn out to be economically viable, but other designs sprang up nearby that are still making the companies that own them lots of money. SCE also built a pilot coal gasification plant at the site. Coal gasification was not new technology even in 1980. The Texaco process SCE used was at least fifty years old at the time and during World War II the Germans had converted coal into gasoline on an industrial scale. All over America innovation was providing solutions—solutions that only depended upon the high price and low availability of imported oil.

Then, with innovation and, more important, capitalist investment reaching an apex, something very interesting happened. The conspiracy theorists will say that the timing was highly suspicious. The price and availability of foreign oil reversed, and America was flooded with cheap oil. Alaska's North Slope came online about this time, which didn't help the alternative energy economy, but primarily it was the Saudis who opened the tap on the new and vulnerable alternative energy industry. This strategy by the oil producers—countries and companies—not only caused the fledgling alternative energy companies to go bust but also cost venture capitalists a lot of money on the deals. This is the ultimate crime for any new industry. The alternative technologies never completely went away; solar, wind, and geothermal survived because the price of oil could never get to zero—and zero is the fuel cost for solar, wind, and geothermal—but the industry was gutted. New technologies need money to become viable and the venture capitalists are the source of this money. If investors lose money on something once, they are doubly cautious the next time around. Energy conservation and alternative energy technologies became as quaint and dated as white, polyester leisure suits—also a big hit after John Travolta danced his way to stardom in *Saturday Night Fever*.

During the summer of 2008, when oil was approaching $150 a barrel, even the liberal-minded campaign of Barack Obama embraced nuclear fission power as part of a so-called all-of-the-above plan. One engineer, a pro–fission power plant guy, said that considering what America has spent on defending its strategic interests in the Middle East it could have built fifty fission power plants (as the French have done) and given every American family a plug-in electric car for free. Then America would no longer have strategic interests in the Middle East.

When I was in college studying physics and chemistry, and waiting in long gas lines, I thought the long-term hope for us all was nuclear fusion, not to be mistaken for nuclear fission. The Fukushima nuclear disaster underscores the risks inherent to fission—if it breaks, it goes out of control. The guys in the chemistry department where I worked talked about fusion all the time. Unlike the nuclear fission power plants we have now, nuclear fusion is inherently safe, the reaction can't run out of control and melt down like Fukushima, and it doesn't produce nuclear waste as a byproduct. The reaction produces the inert gas helium, and best of all...the fuel is *water. I know! What's not to like?*

The problem is that a fusion reaction needs to be very hot. Fusion is what happens in the sun and in a hydrogen bomb, and in the 1970s our technology couldn't create the temperatures needed to maintain the reaction. The challenge was that the heat bled off into the reaction chambers faster than it could be created. My friends and I at the physical sciences kegger parties, held every Friday afternoon in the courtyard of the chemistry department, had the forlorn hope that somehow a magnetic bottle could be created, but we really didn't see how. Fusion was the Holy Grail for us; American ingenuity would find the answer and we wouldn't need foreign oil ever again.

In my first novel, Spirit of Error, completed in 1979, the hero uses a "molecular fusion" bomb to blow up the bad guys.

It turns out that the difficulty in maintaining the temperature is a good thing when you think about it. Our current fission reactors have the scary attribute that if something goes wrong—think Three Mile Island, Chernobyl, and now Fukushima—the reaction proceeds in a frightening and uncontrollable way. A fusion reactor does the exact opposite; it is so difficult to maintain the reaction temperature that if anything goes wrong the reactor shuts down all on its own, without damaging a thing.

The reason I bring up these old memories is that when oil approached $150 per barrel in 2008, the companies that provide alternative energy technologies were making money in the stock market. Solar, wind, natural gas, coal—everything was going up. One day I wondered what had ever happened to nuclear fusion, the one technology that could provide huge amounts of cheap, almost free, energy without generating inconvenient waste products to send to a disposal site or carbon dioxide to screw up the atmosphere. No one seemed to talk about it anymore. So I went online to see what had happened to fusion development over the last thirty or so years. I was stunned.

I was raised to believe in Yankee ingenuity. Who invented the telephone, or the electric light, or powered flight, or cured polio, or...? You get my point. America, since its beginnings, has always been a cauldron of innovation. I think this is because our founding fathers set up the system to reward it; America is a place where innovation can make an individual a lot of money. Free market capitalism creates innovation by rewarding hard work, ambition, and brains. Here is the "but": but, in a modern world, where innovation is very expensive and very risky, a visionary government is needed to nurture the process along. Think about the huge investments America made in the Manhattan Project or the space program or the Internet and the incalculably large returns we got on those investments. America has not had this kind of visionary government—patting the infant of innovation on the diapered rear end—for decades.

When I looked up nuclear fusion on the Internet I found that the European Union (EU) had recently solved the fusion reaction temperature problem with—guess what?—a magnetic bottle, and had reached the Holy Grail of fusion—the energy break-even point. The EU reaction process could finally produce more energy than it needed to maintain the reaction. America had yielded leadership in fusion technology to the Europeans during the administration of president Bill Clinton when they cut the funding for our own fusion research. What has happened to us? Why are all our scientists and engineers coming from abroad? Why has America fallen behind in the innovation race? My opinion is that this is a failure in leadership—political and corporate.

That was in 2008, during the market meltdown. At the time, the EU was actually building a much larger, commercial-size power plant that was planned to be finished and producing profitable electricity by 2010. I was happy the solution was coming, but it broke my heart that America wouldn't lead the effort. Unfortunately, the economic crash brought fusion down with it. The EU cut funding for the fusion-power plant project in January 2011.

The EU project, and fusion technology in general, were again in the leaderless limbo of politics.

Since that time scientists in the United States have increased the yield from controlled fusion tenfold, so now the reaction makes ten times the energy it consumes. They estimate a commercial power plant could be online within ten years. We need to support this effort as we did the Manhattan Project and the Apollo Program.

I was watching a newscast the other night and there was a "happy news" story about an old golden retriever. The old dog had initially been in very bad shape; degradation of its hip joints had made it impossible for the dog to walk or even stand. The treating veterinarian had treated the dog's hip joints with stem cell therapy and there had been startling results. Video showed the dog before and after the treatment—from bedridden to running for a Frisbee. The vet said that they were years ahead in the treatment of animals with stem cell therapy—years ahead of where we are in treating humans. I thought of my mother's arthritis, which had immobilized and tortured her until her death, and what stem cell therapy would have meant to her. I know this is a political hot potato, but my point is that America is falling behind in the innovation race because of political decisions and our politics are out of control.

When it came to an energy policy, it's not like the government did nothing—it did *worse* than nothing. In 2005 I was managing a group of chemical engineers in a large Southern California oil refinery when details of the federal government's ethanol program came out. Remember what chemical engineers do and what they have been educated to do: they make gasoline. They spend every day comparing the engineering economics of fuel and fuel usage. Every chemical engineer I spoke with at the time had the same opinion: the production and use of ethanol as an automotive fuel consumes more imported oil than would be used if the imported oil was refined into gasoline and used in the cars in the first place. It was a no-brainer for chemical engineers. The idea of using low energy food products, grown with hydrocarbon based fertilizers and hydrocarbon driven farm equipment, as fuel was doomed from the start. One of the young and brilliant engineers working for me had the foresight to bring up the question of the environment and the cost of food. His big point was that a government-supported ethanol program would cause the dirt farmers in Brazil to burn even more of the rain forest there in order to plant ethanol-producing crops, thereby aggravating the global warming problem and elevating the price of food. Smart young guy, I'm sure he won't work in the plants as long as I did. For a chemical engineer, the idea of using corn-based ethanol for fuel was a nonstarter, but politically it won't die.

It was great to get that off of my chest, but let me get back to the reason I wrote this book and the reason you are reading it: making money in the stock market. High-priced oil, when we are living in an oil economy, is a killer of investments. The new industries, the alternative energy high fliers when oil is costly—solar, wind, coal, and the rest—seem like a good place to invest when oil is short, but all the oil producers need to do is increase production and the price of oil plummets again. A sudden reduction in the price of oil will again drive our innovative alternative energy companies out of business before they can really get going. Remember what happened in the 1980s and 1990s. Here is where I will utter a word many people, especially investors, won't like: *taxes.*

As I have said before, I am a fiscal conservative. I believe government should not spend money profligately and it should minimize the amount of taxes it takes out of the economic system. Taxes are a necessary evil, but I believe taxes should be minimized whenever possible. *Here it comes.* I also believe we should have an alternative energy defense tax. *Yes, I am recommending a new tax!* How can this be?

Here is how I think an alternative energy defense tax (AEDT) should work: If the price of oil drops precipitously below some level yet to be decided (say $75 per barrel), imported oil will be taxed back up to this floor level. The creation of a floor level in the price of imported oil will allow our fledgling alternative energy industry to perform engineering economics on their ideas. More important, the venture capitalist will invest without fear of being wiped out again. Any pie-in-the-sky idea sounds great if oil is $200 or $300 per barrel, but without a floor in the price, any investment can be wiped out almost overnight. A floor in the price of imported oil will allow investors to calculate a worst-case scenario—what the minimum profit will be for the investment if the price of oil drops to the floor level. If the price of oil does drop and the AEDT takes effect, the proceeds can be used to further invest in our homegrown, domestically produced, alternative energy industry and yes, even in domestic development of carbon-based fuels. Remember, there is no tax until the price of oil drops below the selected price—$75 per barrel in the example above—and the tax is only on imported oil.

I saw a television program recently that detailed the complete rebuilding and modernization of the city of Dubai. It is a spectacular new city that will be the envy of the world. All I could think was, "That is our money they are spending." Recently, during the summer of 2012, the Saudis pumped oil at a breakneck pace and the price of oil dropped to below $80 per barrel—and the solar and wind company stocks were gutted. First Solar, the biggest and best of the American solar companies dropped from above $200 a share to less than $20. Looks like the Saudis won again; by fall of 2013 oil was again well above $100, but our alternative energy companies were still on the ropes.

Here is an oversimplification: more imported oil bad; less imported oil good.

During the summer of 2012 oil was down again, but gasoline prices continued to rise. The reason was the oil companies had shut down refining capacity. If they don't make gas, because they feel their margins are not high enough, the availability—the supply—of gasoline decreases and the price of gasoline increases. This manipulation of the price is the same thing that Enron did to the price of electricity in California, artificially elevating the price by shutting down power plants. Should this be legal? Shutting off the gas spigot is like turning off the drinking water for Californians and indeed all Americans. Gasoline and heating oil are utilities, not commodities. Maybe we need a bid system for refining capacity.

Here is how a bid system could work. Companies that make and sell fuel would be required by law to estimate their refining volumes at the beginning of the year. So oil companies would estimate their refinery throughput, the total number of gallons of gas and heating oil they are going to produce during the coming year—they already do this as a part of their planning. Their minimum tax burden would come to them if they hit their estimate right on the number; if there were deviations on either side of the estimate, lower or higher production, the tax subsidy would decrease. No more shutting down the refining capacity to drive up the price of gas at the pump.

This system would be self-regulating. If an oil company wants to provide this critical utility to the public it has to play. If it wants the big money during the good times, when actual high demand for the fuel drives up the prices and the margins, it had better have a healthy forecast. If it tries to sandbag its forecast by estimating too low, it could still sell all the product it could make, but there would be an increased tax to pay on volumes above the sandbagged estimate.

The details would need to be fair to the refiners too; their risk could even be hedged by tagging it to gross domestic product or some other measurement of economic demand to avoid having them trapped by radically changing economic conditions beyond their control. Oil companies would still be able to make more or less than the amount they predicted, but artificially created shortages to drive up prices and increase margins would cost more than it would be worth. If they produce less or more than they have said they will produce, they will pay the tax on the missed forecast. This would bring the artificial mismatch between supply and demand into balance.

When I ran my AEDT idea by my newsletter readers, most liked the idea, but one critic asked about the so-called double taxation problem. This complaint states that after companies pay taxes on profits the same profits are taxed again when stockholders pay taxes on the dividends they receive. Well, yes, but this argument really doesn't hold water—the profits go to separate entities. When General Motors buys a part, the part supplier pays tax on the sale and when GM sells the car with the part inside GM pays tax on the car sold. Is the part taxed twice? Yes, but that is the system. But I understand my critic's frustration. The system would be better if dividends were all taxed the way master limited partnerships are taxed. After all, if a shareholder is really an owner, then the corporate tax deductions should accompany the profits when the shareholder is taxed.

Some say oil slumped because of a weak euro, but I think it is more related to the dollar being strong. I listened to one of the talking heads on CNBC, an oil industry analyst, who said not to worry over recent increased tension between the United States and Iran, or Israel and Iran, or missiles and nuke production. He was "talking his book," the book of the warmonger, the war profiteer, the oil interests, and Dwight D. Eisenhower's military-industrial complex. "It is easier for us to replace Iranian oil than it is for Iran to replace imported gasoline," he said, "and compared to the US Navy, the Iranian navy is inconsequential."

Another guy on the show said, "Everyone knows that if Iran tries to block the Straits of Hormuz they will lose both their navy and air force in the first hour or two."

It reminds me of what happened in 1941, after the United States cut off oil shipments to industrialized Japan; a Japan that was at war in China and considered oil imports critical to national survival. The last thing the first expert said was, "Oil would spike $30 or $40, but it would be temporary." You could almost see him mentally counting the profits he would make on that spike.

My questions to the war profiteers are, "And if they blow up an A-bomb in the desert? What then, war hawks? How do you attack them then? How did our politics and military stance with North Korea change once it got the bomb?"

Since North Korea became a nuclear player, we have left it pretty much alone; no more saber rattling with the North Koreans. The lesson learned by all petty totalitarian regimes is, "Get the bomb as soon as possible." Many of these petty dictatorships believe having the bomb is the only way to get an intrusive and warlike United States to back off. Since 1941 the United States has been involved in more than forty wars in other people's countries. In many parts of the world, when local people are polled they say, unfortunately, that America is the number one threat to peace.

I, for one, am a little tired of America being policeman to an ungrateful world.

Chapter 10

What Happened to the Markets?

Rational-Market Theory: Humans Being Humans a Surprise?

In Erich Von Stroheim's 1924 silent movie *Greed*, love and friendship fall victim to the dehumanizing lust for money. The opening title card reads:

GOLD—GOLD—GOLD—GOLD
Bright and Yellow, Hard and Cold, Molten, Graven, Hammered,
Rolled, Hard to Get and Light to Hold; Stolen, Borrowed,
Squandered—Doled.

Best friends McTeague (Gibson Gowland) and Marcus (Jean Hersholt) have a friendship that is strong enough to survive even after Marcus's girl, Trina (ZaSu Pitts), falls in love with McTeague, and they are married. But after Trina wins a big lottery prize of $5,000 the three devolve into the basest forms of humanity. Trina becomes so miserly that she won't spend any of the lottery money, preferring to live in poverty and squalor; gazing lovingly at her gold coins she says, "How I've slaved and starved for you." McTeague loses his job and descends into drunkenness and violence. And Marcus can't stop thinking that had he kept Trina as his own, *he* would have the $5,000. After many degrading episodes— the original movie was over eight hours long—the lust for money drives McTeague to torture and murder Trina and flee into Death Valley with the treasure. Marcus, also still obsessed with the money, finally catches up to McTeague in the hell-like heat of the desert. *Home sweet home!* Out of water and with their mule dead, cooperation is their only hope to escape the heat of the desert, but instead they fight a final struggle over the money, with McTeague brutally pistol-whipping Marcus to death, saying, "Even if we're done for, I'll take some o' my truck along." But during the struggle, Marcus has somehow managed to handcuff their hands together. Finally in sole possession of the money littering the dry sand around him, handcuffed to the body of his old friend, McTeague faces the horror of Death Valley alone.

***

Remember the old story of the scorpion and the frog? It goes something like this. Separately, a frog and a scorpion walk up to a running river. Just as the frog is starting into the river to cross, the scorpion says, "Hey, wait a minute. I can't swim. Why don't you give me a ride across this river?" The frog replies, "Because you will sting me and we will both drown." But the scorpion explains why that would not be rational. Why would he sting the frog? The sting would also cause him to die. So the frog agrees and the scorpion hops on. They are about halfway across the river when sure enough, the scorpion stings the frog. The frog looks back in surprise and asks, "Why did you do that? Now we are both going to die." The scorpion replies, "Hey, you knew I was a scorpion when I got on. That is what I do."

During the lead-up to the banking crisis, when the investment banks ran up sixty-to-one leverage in a one-sided trade without rational concern about the impact of their actions should they be wrong (see the risk matrix, in chapter 4), they—"Wall Street" in New York and "The City" in London—played the role of the scorpion that stung the frog as they crossed the river. Who was the frog? It was all the believers in the efficient and rational-market theories—and us, for letting them call the shots.

The efficient-market hypothesis is not a new theory; it dates back to the late nineteenth century, but it gained new popularity in the 1960s when the University of Chicago became its champion. It says, in its simplest sense, that prices on anything traded will reflect all publicly available information. It was all the vogue until the 1990s when the behavioral finance economists spoiled the fun by using actual market performance to dispute the efficient-market model—funny how the facts can screw up a great theory. The rational-market theory, which stems from the efficient-market hypothesis, says that the expectations of "agents" will be the same as the statistical true expectation—that is, the guys placing the bets will have the same expectations that the facts tell them they should have. Tut-tut; anyone who has ever watched the odds board at the racetrack could tell the theorists that this is not true. Once again, the facts showed that people will be people and will do irrational things.

The argument between those who believe in rational markets and those who do not reminds me of the debate that has raged in quantum physics since the beginning of the theory. The old understanding of quantum mechanics had Schrödinger's cat in a superstate where it was both alive and dead at the same time. A new interpretation using Bayesian probabilities eliminates the paradox. In Schrödinger's mind experiment, the cat is in a closed box with deadly poison and a poison release mechanism that depends on the random decay of a radioactive element. If the random event happens, the cat dies; if not, it lives. In the old understanding, the fact that we don't know the outcome places the cat in the simultaneously dead and alive superstate. In quantum Bayesianism it is not the cat that is in the superstate, it is our understanding. The cat is either dead or alive; it is our *opinion* of the outcome that is confused. It is the same in the markets: the value of a company does not change based on whether an agent uses all of the available information to price it or not, but the price of the stock does. In quantum mechanical terms, the *opinions* of the humans trading an equity drives price discovery, which is not the same thing as the actual value of the equity.

Members of the administration of president George W. Bush and Republican presidential candidates since have said, "Shame on Wall Street greed for the levels of leverage they built into their investments"—levels of leverage, as high as sixty to one, that made the financial crash of 2008 inevitable. "It is all their fault," they rationalized.

Yet the Bush appointee Christopher Cox, former chairman of the Securities and Exchange Commission (SEC), had a critical role in making the crash possible. Here is his record:

- In 2003, Cox voided the short-sale uptick rule—a rule put in place after the hard lessons of 1929, a rule that controlled the short seller's scorpion nature by making it impossible to drive a stock down simply because of light buying interest.

- In 2004, Cox voided the leverage limit (twelve to one) on large investment banks, a rule instituted during the banking crisis of the 1970s that protected bankers from their own greed by limiting the amount they could borrow to bet.

- Then, during the heyday of the no-regulation-is-good rational-market theorists, who then controlled the Bush administration's economic policy, the SEC refused to enforce the naked short-sell rules when they were unable to find a way to void them. This rule simply states that a firm needs to own or borrow the stock they want to short before they can sell it. This is to maintain a balance between the number of shares outstanding and the number of shares sold. On the Friday before Lehman Brothers failed (September 12, 2008) there were three times the number of shorts on Sears Holdings as there were shares in existence.

During the height of the banking crisis, almost all the senators on the Republican side of the aisle fought tooth and nail against the Bush administration's so-called bailout plan. They didn't seem to realize that it was their own party's policies that had caused the mess in the first place. Afterward, all the market gurus and egghead professors agreed that had the bank bailout not come through, both Goldman Sachs and Morgan Stanley would also have gone bankrupt and the global banking system would have been destroyed.

But what was the huge bet the investment bankers had borrowed so much to leverage up sixty to one to put on? Well, that brings us back to Wall Street and financial engineering. Financial engineering, or computational finance, has been defined as a "field that relies on computational intelligence, mathematical finance, numerical methods, and computer simulations to make trading, hedging, and investment decisions, as well as facilitating the risk management of those decisions." Garbage in, garbage out. If all these mathematical constructs depend on the belief that no one will put on a bet that could possibly harm them—rational-market theory—you get what we got: disaster.

When Alan Greenspan, one of the world's biggest proponents of the rational-market theory before the crash, testified before Congress, he said he had "made a mistake in presuming" that financial firms could regulate themselves. "Those of us who have looked to the self-interest of lending institutions to protect shareholders' equity, myself included, are in a state of shocked disbelief," he said when testifying before the House Oversight Committee. Greenspan believed that the markets would always correct imbalance—even if the imbalance was created by fraud—and therefore the government should not regulate the markets. We saw in his congressional testimony just how naive he had been.

But we can't just blame the deluded followers of Ayn Rand and the rational-market theory. We need to look at the foundations of American values—values that put making money above almost anything else. We need to look at ourselves...and the scorpion stinging the frog: "You knew I was a scorpion when I got on."

Since the economic boom began in 1982, America has sent its best and brightest to Wall Street. These young people, the smartest of each graduating class, were told the rules of Reaganomics:

- Rule #1—Make as much money as you can, as fast as you can.

- Rule #2—There is no Rule #2.

The miracle of Laffer Curve economics is that the more wealth you acquire, the more wealth will trickle down to the less gifted. Deficits don't matter, so let's borrow as much as we can to reduce taxes at the top. "Voodoo economics" is how George H. W. Bush described it—history's view of this one-term president becomes rosier every year.

In the beginning of the boom, Wall Street amounted to about 17 percent of America's gross domestic product. At the time of the crash, Wall Street was over 60 percent. Our smartest young people grew up on Wall Street over the past thirty years in a system that praised and rewarded scorpions. Our government created the Wild Wild West environment experienced on Wall Street during the last thirty years. Reaganomics and the rational-market theory stated clearly that *all* regulation was bad, and most of the hard-learned lessons of the 1930s were cast aside. During the years of president Bill Clinton, too! Our best and brightest graduates weren't born scorpions; the work and the regulatory framework in which they operated forced them to morph into them or perish.

I wish one of the Goldman Sachs or American International Group (AIG) guys would have stood up at one of these congressional hearings and said, "Hey, you guys knew we were scorpions when we got on." He might add, "In fact, we weren't even scorpions until that was what you required us to become."

Congress and their circus-like hearings are as distasteful as the Wall Street excesses. Anyone who doesn't understand that there are two sides to every trade, a buyer and a seller—even on trades as crazy as AIG writing hundreds of billions of dollars in credit default swaps on doomed and overleveraged Lehman Brothers debt—should not be in Congress. And whose fault is it that these uninformed people are running our government? Ours—we are the voters who put them there.

The Power and Danger of Derivatives

Many financial instruments have been grouped into the catchall category of "derivatives." Stock options are derivatives; they are derived from the underlying value of the stocks on which the contracts are based. They provide the powerful and valuable capacity to insure our stock positions against loss.

A simple definition of derivatives is that they are contracts between two parties with different beliefs about the direction of the underlying asset. In addition to stock options, there are futures, credit default swaps (CDSs), and many others. The problem with derivatives is that they can become highly leveraged. This high leverage can be, as we have seen from the stock options market and the real estate market, a very good thing; but as we learned when the CDS market went belly-up, unreasonably high leverage can also be very, very dangerous. What made the CDS market so massively dangerous was the total lack of transparency in which the swaps were traded; few realized how overextended the world had become until the crash came. Warren Buffet's famous statement that derivatives were "financial weapons of mass destruction" did not prevent him from buying and selling millions of dollars worth of them. It reminds me of the old saying in golf: "It's not the club, it's the golfer." What is needed is just a little bit of regulation to make sure the scorpions don't sting the frog; and a transparent CDS market, like the options market.

There was a time when if you wanted to buy a house you went to a bank, proved your income, proved your credit worthiness, and put down 20 percent as a down payment. But during the first six or seven years after the 2000 elections, the smart guys on Wall Street came up with a new instrument that would, as they explained it, diminish the risk of issuing a risky mortgage, and would produce an entirely new stream of liquidity for home mortgages. A wonder weapon. In a very oversimplified explanation—I'm just a flea after all—here is how they did it.

The creative financial engineers bundled up thousands of risky mortgages with thousands of good mortgages and used the baskets of mortgage loans as the income stream for bonds they sold on Wall Street. They added up the earning potential of the baskets based on the sum of what each mortgage would earn for the loan owner, divided this pie into as many bonds as they thought they could sell, and put them on the market. These were the now famous mortgage-backed securities (MBSs). But, you may ask, the bonds still contained risky mortgages, so who in their right mind would buy them? Well, the Wall Street guys hired some very smart mathematicians to figure out some complicated formulas that would spread the risk...they thought.

It all seemed reasonable; but it becomes much more complicated when the way they buried high-risk mortgages under the low-risk ones is considered. This practice was how they received artificially high credit ratings for these bonds.

The purchasers of the new MBS bonds would own a share of the mortgage pie. Baked into the pie were the costs of the original mortgages. To get the loans, in order to bundle them up, the Wall Street bankers bought them from the loan companies that had loaned us the money to buy our homes. The cost the bankers paid included the amount the original loan company had loaned out (the principal) plus the interest the loan would earn over its duration. The bankers could then create a bond that would pay this interest out to the new bondholders. Potential bond purchasers liked the high yield the bond would pay, but were concerned about the amount paid out for the original loan principal. The cost of the bond would necessarily include a share of this money loaned out. If the value of the underlying real estate went down, the potential bond purchasers thought, the borrower might not pay off the mortgage as agreed and the bond would lose this share of the loan principal, the amount originally borrowed. The bankers didn't find many buyers for these bonds; the risk of default was just too great.

The answer the bankers were seeking came in the form of insurance. They could write an insurance policy, for a price, that would guarantee full payment of the loan principal. Of course the bankers didn't want to get stuck with this risk either, so they did what they did best: they created more bonds to sell. These second-level bonds swapped the risk from the MBS bonds to a new insurance type instrument, the credit default swap (CDS). (The first modern CDS contract was created by JP Morgan in 1994 when they loaned money to Exxon after the Exxon Valdez coated Prince William sound with oil.) The bankers could now sell the MBS bonds easily if they were paired up with the CDSs. The great part for the bankers was that CDSs could also be sold and they could take another slice from the pie. By grouping high-risk mortgages with low-risk mortgages the banksters were able to get the MBS bonds AAA ratings, however bogus the ratings turned out to be in the end. With the MBS bonds holding AAA ratings, the risk of default was thought to be minuscule, and the amount of money to be made was huge, so the demand for the MBS bonds was high—as long as they could be paired with the CDSs.

If you buy a million dollars' worth of life insurance, you pay a premium to get it, and the insurance company is happy to take it. Unlike a car or a house that has a fixed, insurable value, you can even buy more life insurance. You can double up and buy another million dollars' worth of life insurance if you are willing to pay the premium. This same thing happened in the CDS market. There was no limit to the amount of times someone could buy a CDS as long as someone else would sell the premium and take on the risk of default (think AIG). Since the market was unregulated, you didn't even need to be associated with the original MBS bond to buy a CDS. You could insure something you didn't own! It is like taking out life insurance on a stranger. Somewhere between forty and sixty times the value of the original MBS bonds was ultimately insured by CDSs. If the MBS bonds defaulted on the interest payment to the owners, the writers of the CDSs—the insurance companies and others who had accepted the premiums and taken on the risk—would owe forty to sixty times the value of the insured loans. Eventual implosion was inevitable.

When mortgages began to be foreclosed and the MBS bonds began to falter, the sharks bought even more CDSs. If the MBS bonds defaulted, the sharks got paid the principal in multiples of how many CDSs they'd purchased. They *wanted* the MBS bonds to default. The sharks knew that if they bought a lot of them, the CDS price, the price of insurance, would go up—the insurance companies would want more money to take on the increasing risk. The sharks also knew that the increasing CDS prices would signal the market that the companies holding the MBS bonds were in trouble and that this would drive down the price of their common stock. It was a beautiful thing for the sharks. They paid for the CDSs they bought by selling short the stock of companies they knew they could manipulate to lower prices. They made money from both trades—on paper—as the stock market melted down. But who was going to pay them the astounding multiples of the principal? Maybe the liability was so large that no one could pay.

The mortgage bond CDS market is dead and along with it died the MBS trade, and this was not good for the housing market. When the Troubled Asset Relief Program (TARP) bill was passed, no one knew if the CDSs were worthless or not. In the end, most of the CDSs were closed out at much less than face value, sometimes thirty cents on the dollar. So even the sharks got skinned and fried.

Eventually, with our banking system on the rocks and AIG, the biggest writer of the credit default obligations (the swaps), going down fast, you and I paid the sixtyfold principal on mountains of bad mortgage-backed securities. Our government still owned a huge share of AIG in late 2012.

To make things even more complicated, the MBS bonds the Wall Street guys sold, based on the same basket of mortgages, were not all the same and did not have the same risk. Their complex algorithms calculated the chances of each mortgage in the basket going into default, and the mix of good loans to bad loans in the basket, to come up with a theoretical value of the bond. Then they created several levels of bonds that differed mainly in the promise made to repay the bond buyer's investment—who would get paid first in the event the mortgages in the basket were not paid and the MBS bonds went bad.

Each of these baskets of mortgages was different and the bonds created to fund them were one of a kind and very complex. To keep this explanation simple, let's split the basket into three levels of bonds. The highest-level bonds, the ones that gave the new owner the right to the first money out, were sold with AAA ratings. The bond-rating agencies went right along with this idea, but then the rating agencies made their money from the guys creating the bonds in the first place. This is roughly analogous to the health department guy who rates food establishments getting paid directly by the restaurant owners—in cash.

The AAA rating assured the bond buyer that the bond would always pay up. Then the guys who had bundled up the mortgages sold some more bonds that gave the owner the second bite of the apple in the case of default. These bonds would necessarily pay a higher interest rate because they had higher risk and would be rated, theoretically, with a lower rating—say, BB. Finally, they sold the last group of bonds, the bonds that would pay the bondholders last, as so-called junk bonds. These bonds, which gave the owner almost nothing if the mortgages went south, paid very high interest rates, but were assigned, theoretically, much lower ratings—say, C. The lower-rated bonds—the higher-risk bonds—paid correspondingly higher interest rates to attract buyers. So far so good—higher risk, higher return; lower risk, lower return.

This is how bonds work. The beauty of the MBS bond was also its flaw: all the variously rated bonds were based on the same basket of loans.

To get reasonable people to buy these new products, the Wall Street guys sold them CDS insurance on their bonds. The CDS contract stated that if the bond ever failed to pay the interest, the entity insuring the bond would pay the principal; thus taking on the risk of the bond's default. Sounded good, but the basis of it all was still the very risky mortgages inside the basket of loans. First time the bond interest payment is missed the CDS owner gets paid the entire principal of the loan—as many times over as they have bought the CDS.

The Wall Street guys are smart. They make their living by betting on risk, good and bad. It was only a matter of time before they would bite the hand that fed them or, to maintain the analogy, sting the frog. We have since found out that the same guys who were creating the bonds were betting against them by buying the CDSs on them. In fact, the really smart guys were working with the bond creators to make sure there were enough really, really bad mortgages in the basket to ensure that the bond would fail. The mechanism for this was that the bond needs an initial investor to put up a tiny portion of the value of the bond. The smart guys would tell the bond guys (think Lehman Brothers) that they would make that initial investment in the equity if they could make sure the bond was packed full of loans sure to fail. Once the doomed bond was created, they indeed funded the equity tranche, but then they went out and bought the CDSs on the very same bond—over and over and over and over. And AIG sold the CDSs to them—over and over and over and over—thereby taking on the liability of the principal of the bond forty or fifty or sixty times over. Not very rational—not for AIG, anyway.

The credit default swaps were traded freely in a shadowy, unregulated, over-the-counter marketplace. As noted above, CDSs are contracts that guarantee the principal on the mortgage bonds if the bonds were to default on the interest payment. The CDSs traded independently of the underlying bonds. It is analogous to going to Las Vegas and betting on a football game. Someone bets a team will win and someone else bets the team will lose. The bets are independent of the game and of the teams actually playing the game. The bet you place does not affect the outcome of the game. This is where the hedge funds came into the mix. Hedge funds were also unregulated and were very secretive.

What the hedge funds were able to do is to select a bank that had become weakened by owning too many of the mortgage bonds. Betting, in secret, that the weakened bank's stock would go down, they sold the stock at a lower price than it was going for at the time. This is the "short selling" you have heard so much about. When they sold the stock they got the money in exchange for a promise to produce the stock at the lower price at some later date. They were betting that they would be able to buy the stock back at an even lower price.

This is when the guys betting on the game actually began to affect the outcome of the game. They took the money they had received from the short sale of the stock, went to the CDS market, and bought the CDSs on the bonds the bank had in its account. By buying insurance against the default of the bonds they were making a statement to the marketplace, anonymously, that the bonds were at risk. By buying a lot of them, they drove the cost of this insurance—the price of the CDSs—up and the price of the stock down. This increasing price of insuring the bonds told the market that the bank was at increasing risk of going broke.

In Vegas, the more people bet a team will lose, the more the odds will telegraph that will indeed be the case. As more people bet the team will lose, the odds the team will lose go up, and the cost of placing the bet goes up in terms of how much the bet will pay out in the case of the loss. But in sports betting, the wagering does not affect the outcome of the game; unless, of course, we are talking about the true story of the Chicago "Black" Sox, who famously threw the 1919 World Series. In 1988 the story was made into the movie *Eight Men Out*; written and directed by John Sayles, the film starred John Cusack as Buck Weaver and D. B. Sweeney as Shoeless Joe Jackson.

But if the team happens to be a bank that depends on the trust of the marketplace, the bet becomes a self-fulfilling prophecy. The market sees the price of the CDS going up, and the stock price decreases; the betting actually affects the outcome of the game. The hedge funds make out on both trades: the CDS prices going up and the bank stock price going down. The more the trade works, the more the hedge funds will pile into it. Then if someone in a hedge fund happens to start a rumor that that bank has problems (the quarterback has a bad knee), the process becomes a monster. In late 2008, the stocks of the banks holding the mortgage bonds plummeted and the CDS prices soared. Finally, as in the cases of Bear Stearns and Lehman Brothers, the banks failed, making the hedge funds even more money when the CDS contracts came due. Of course the issuer of the CDSs, AIG, didn't have the money to pay the sixtyfold liability, so good old Uncle Sam needed to come in and save the day in the form of TARP.

Here is how I explained the credit default swap market in my January 29, 2009, newsletter, when I was jumping up and down on the desk demanding they be nationalized—thereby denying the bad guys their profits.

In a Main Street analogy, this process would look something like this. Say a guy owns a restaurant and bar. His business is doing well, so he decides to buy a big new house based on his expectations that the business will continue to grow. If Main Street were to operate like Wall Street:

- There would be a market where someone unrelated to the restaurant owner could buy home-mortgage insurance on the restaurateur's new house, betting he won't pay his new mortgage.

- It would be legal for someone to sell his house without actually owning it, receiving payment now for the promise to produce the house when the sales contract demanded it in the future.

At this point in the Main Street analogy, in swoops the alcohol distribution company (like the hedge fund) that sells the restaurant owner his beer and wine. The distribution company sells the restaurant owner's house for a very public and very low price at the same time they start buying insurance on the guy's mortgage. Both of these things lower the value of his house, but the worst is yet to come. Second, the distribution company refuses to deliver any alcohol to the guy's restaurant, saying his credit has become worse due to the lower value of his house and the increased risk that he can't pay his mortgage, as indicated by the increased cost of the mortgage insurance. Since the restaurateur's beer and wine sales are a major part of his business, his profits drop dramatically. Then say that someone in the alcohol distribution company starts a rumor that someone has gotten food poisoning at the restaurant. The owner's restaurant business drops to zero. The owner can't pay his mortgage, and the price of the mortgage insurance increases, allowing the distributor to sell it off at a big profit. The price of the house plummets, allowing the distributor to buy it for pennies on the dollar before he needs to produce it in fulfillment of his sale contract. The final result is lots of fast profits for the alcohol distributor and lots of pain for the poor restaurant owner.

But is it the really the end of the disaster? To whom is the alcohol distributor going to sell alcohol now? Now imagine that the truck leasing company, whom the alcohol distributor depends on to deliver his product, notices that the alcohol distributor's business has taken a downturn. After all, there is one less restaurant out there to buy his booze. Now the truck leasing company starts the same murderous process on the alcohol distributor as the distributor used to destroy the restaurant owner. It doesn't take long for the process to spin out of control.

The hedge fund and brokerage companies that were playing this scorpion trade owned a lot of the toxic paper themselves. The rating guys who gave the stock ratings on big brokerage houses kept lowering their estimates on each other's stock price. One television commentator said, "This is like children saying, I know you are, but what am I?" In the end they all lost their shirts.

One big bond manager explained the credit crunch this way. When you drive up to a fast-food restaurant, you place your order, and then drive around. On the other side of the building are two windows; at the first window you pay for your order and at the second window you pick up your burgers. It is a matter of trust. The fast-food place starts cooking your burgers when you place your order because they trust that you will pay for it on the other side of the building. You pay for it because you trust that when you drive up to the next window you will get your order. If this trust is lost, as it was lost in the global credit markets in 2008, you may get to the payment window and not pay, doubting that the burgers will actually be at the next window—causing the burgers to rot. The other side of the coin is that the restaurant may not want to cook your burgers when you order, because they doubt that you will pay. You go hungry and business at the fast-food place "freezes up," as did our global credit markets.

In my February 13, 2009, investment newsletter I went into much more detail to explain how the CDS market was structured. I said, "OK, I know it's complicated, but it is important." Here is the explanation in its entirety:

Level 1—Home loans. These are good things; they provide capital for home ownership. In the good old days, you needed to be able to pay for a loan before you could get one. But with waves of cheap money flowing from Wall Street after 2002, the standards dropped—during the boom, you needed only to have a pulse.

Level 2—Mortgage-backed securities (MBSs). These are also good things; they provide capital for home loans and have predictable risk and stable, long-term returns to the people who buy them. Like any other type of bond, the market price is a compromise between the interest paid and the risk taken. Say there are one thousand mortgages that, when taken together, have a total principal of $350 million. The principal is the total value of the houses when the loans were made (average house price of $350,000). These loans, taken together, have an average interest rate payment of, say, 12 percent. The Wall Street bankers might have divided the package of loans into 3,500,000 bonds, selling at $100 each and paying an interest rate of 12 percent. But that is not what they did, because it was not enough profit for them. You can bet when they split these up into CDO bonds (see below), the amount they made was far greater than if they had simply sold the MBS bonds on the original $350 million.

These average interest rates sound high, but remember, many of the loans that were bundled together were of the subprime variety. These loans had very high rates on the first mortgage and astronomically high rates on second mortgages taken out to pay the down payment. As always in bonds—and everything else, for that matter—the higher the risk, the higher the interest rate needs to be to entice buyers. This is all as it should be. A bond rating on these instruments should be relatively simple to generate. Before the crisis, 97 percent of all the outstanding mortgages were being paid on time so the rating could be high—say AAA. The catch is that the first loans likely to default are the most profitable—the high interest subprime variety.

Level 3—Collateralized debt obligations (CDOs). These things are where the problem and the sleight of hand begin. These instruments were developed from the MBS bonds described above. How can you make another financial instrument from an MBS? The principal value is set and the interest rate is set (or at least known) and the risk is averaged for all the underlying loans. Well, the MBS bonds were not sold as a unit. They were divided up into pieces that were sold with variations in the repayment terms that changed the perceived risk. For the sake of simplicity, let's say that the MBS bond was divided into three chunks. All three chunks are based on the original mortgages, but the repayment terms are different for each. The top (senior) chunk has terms that say that if anything goes wrong, the owners of these CDO bonds get their money out first. The owners of the next level down get their money second, if there is any money left. The owners of the bottom slice get their money out last—maybe. So the top slice, based on risk, would be more expensive to buy and pay a lower interest rate. The bottom slice would be cheaper to buy and pay a higher interest rate. There is still logic in this creative instrument: lower risk, lower return, and higher risk, higher return. The problem arose when these instruments were rated by the bond rating agencies. One would expect that the senior slice would get an AAA rating and the slices below would receive much lower bond ratings. The bond rating companies, such as Moody's, say now that they rated these bonds based on the way they were performing during the real estate boom—none of the MBS bonds were failing, so most of the CDO bonds were safe. So as many as 85 percent of the CDO bonds received AAA bond ratings, predicting little or no risk, even though a good percentage of the loans packaged into the MBS bonds were subprime and, more important, a huge percentage of the yield was due to the very profitable high-risk mortgages. Oh, and the rating agencies were getting paid by the Wall Street bankers who created the CDO bonds, so it behooved them to give them high ratings if they wanted future business. These things were sold all over the world as money-good bonds.

The phony, artificially high bond ratings given these bonds by the bond rating agencies were one root cause of the final collapse. Iceland went bankrupt because of the AAA CDO bonds they bought from us, and the bonds didn't do the rest of Europe much good either.

Level 4—Credit default swaps (CDSs or "swaps"). These instruments seemed to be a good idea originally. The problem the Wall Street bankers had when trying to sell the CDO bonds was that potential buyers were still concerned that the risk of mortgage default was still too high, even if the bonds had AAA ratings. So the bankers invented a new type of "insurance," called credit default swaps, to protect CDO buyers from the risk of default. The terms of a swap could be anything really, but most were based on a simple concept: if the original MBS bond ever failed to pay the interest promised, the owner of the swap could demand repayment of the principal underlying the MBS. So the CDO buyer could buy the CDO and buy the CDS, thereby earning the high interest on the CDO less the premium paid on the CDS—the difference being a sweet profit—and have the at-risk principal insured. Makes sense to me. If the MBS failed to pay the promised interest, the insurer (seller of the swap) was obligated to go out into the market and buy the MBS and provide it to the swap owner—or pay the difference in cash.

The problem was that the people buying the credit default swaps didn't need to buy the CDO. They didn't need to have an interest in the MBS or the CDO; they could simply speculate on the failure of the MBS. They could do this over and over and over again. Since the MBS bonds were AAA rated, and they could make lots of money in swap premiums, the companies writing (selling) the swaps (AIG, Citigroup, Lehman Brothers, Bear Stearns, and others) kept on writing the insurance even when their liability was forty or sixty times the original amount of the MBS bonds. If the MBS bonds defaulted, they would never be able to go out into the market and buy the MBS bonds they owed, because they owed sixty times as many as existed.

The CDSs—the swaps—became essentially valueless. The owners of the swaps could not be paid because the writers of the swaps were insolvent—when the swap liability was included in their balance sheets. So the net effect of all the swap deals was that the banks were, for all practical purposes, bankrupt and the hedge fund sharks who bought the swaps were all out the premiums they paid to buy them. That was until the Bush administration's TARP money went out to AIG and quickly flowed out the back door to pay the CDS holders; Goldman Sachs was a huge winner that day.

But no one wanted to acknowledge the truth. The $15 trillion owed on the swaps showed up on the swap buyers' financial statements as a gain, although they would ultimately receive only pennies on the dollar, and it showed up on the swap sellers' financial statements as a loss, although they refused to own up to just how big their losses were. All these big financial companies played it both ways; they wrote the swaps and they bought swaps on other companies. The web of interrelated counterparty obligations was a tangled ball of wet string. At the time I didn't think anyone would ever be able to untangle it and said we needed to get out the scissors and start cutting the Gordian knot.

Before Alan Greenspan's reign at the Federal Reserve, these financial instruments were a tiny part of the market, almost nonexistent. From the perspective of a country boy from the desert, it seemed that the solution was obvious: make the swaps go away. All these companies generated huge amounts of liability from selling the swaps and tremendous paper profits from buying other swaps. And none of them wanted to be the one to admit that the value of these things was zero. So instead of declaring them worthless, or nationalizing them, the United States government—you and I—made them money-good.

If all the swaps not paired to the underlying MBS bonds had simply gone away, all the phony earnings and all the phony debt would have evaporated. Who would be out the money? Who knows? You owe me and I owe you and you owe him and he owes me and…you get the idea. But ultimately, the amount really lost would be the premiums paid to buy the swaps—again, pennies on the dollar. That's too bad. That's speculation.

So where did the first $350 billion in TARP payout go? When the banks got the money, it went out the back door to pay down swap liability. But there wasn't enough money in the world to cover all these phony liabilities. This money was wasted; worse, it rewarded the sharks who bought the swaps for speculation and brought the system down.

If the overleveraged swaps had gone away, if we had just said that all the swaps were invalid unless paired with a CDO, the values of the CDO bonds would have again reflected the values within the MBS bonds, which in turn reflected the value of the underlying mortgages—and 97 percent of the mortgages were getting paid. The values of most of the CDO bonds would have skyrocketed. The bottom slices of the pie, the slices that get paid last, might not have fared too well, but that is why the owners of these slices got the highest interest rates—these are very, very risky bonds, the ones that needed the CDS insurance the most. We know that now, in spite of the artificially high bond ratings they once held. Once the dust had cleared there would have been a few big losers, but everyone's balance sheet would have been a lot better off. So why didn't the government void these poisonous swaps? Can you say "Washington lobbyists?"

When a rumor circulated that the government would subsidize the very worst mortgages, radically reducing the number of subprime mortgages that move into default, the Dow Jones Industrial Average bounced 250 points. Government subsidies would reduce the risk in the MBS bonds and concomitantly the risk to the bottom slices of the CDO bonds, but we would've gotten to the same place if the swaps contracts had been voided. The owners of the swaps would not get their windfall and the swap buyers would still be out the premiums they paid, but the markets would have healed. And if the government wanted to be very generous, and I didn't think it should be, they could have reimbursed the sharks who bought the swaps for the premiums they paid out, a fraction of their face value.

The question was, and I suppose still is, which way to this end point was the least expensive for taxpayers? The answer is not clear, but it seems to me that if the downward pressure on the mortgage-backed securities had been removed by voiding the swaps, the housing credit market could have healed and the downward trend in home prices could have been broken much earlier. Homeowners would have gained in two ways, avoiding home value depreciation and not paying taxes to bail out either the subprime mortgage holders or the sharks.

After I wrote these opinions in my newsletter, the real estate market continued its horrific decline for four more years. To show the overwhelming complexity of the swaps market, I have attached a description of how swaps are priced in the "Useful Stuff" section at the end of this book.

The justification for saving the swaps market, as late as the Greek credit crisis of 2012, was that the interest rates paid on bonds, the cost of borrowing, would increase if there were not swaps to defer the risk of the bond. That makes sense if the swaps are matched with the underlying bond. When the Greek bonds were liquidated and the swaps were triggered, we discovered that the sharks had had time to get out of the way of the tsunami before it hit, unlike what had happened when Lehman suddenly went bankrupt. The sellers of the CDSs had not sold sixty times the value of the bonds. The Europeans had learned from our mistakes, and the market had worked, as Greenspan had hoped, although it was four years late for AIG, Lehman, the American banks, and the US homeowner and the American taxpayer.

On April 16, 2010, news broke that the SEC had filed fraud charges against Goldman Sachs, and we got more of the picture. There is a bigger story here regarding the hedge funds that drove the CDO and CDS markets. One of the most fascinating hedge funds was Magnetar Capital; it played the gap in the rules the best and made the most money. Let's return to the Main Street analogy from above.

Lately we have learned that the alcohol distribution company in my example (the hedge fund in the CDS world) has had a special relationship since the very beginning with the building contractor that built the restaurant owner's house (Goldman Sachs). Hedge funds made the original mortgage-backed securities possible in the first place by buying the riskiest part of the MBS, the equity. The equity tranche is a very small portion of the bond—maybe 10 percent—but if this tranche is not sold, the bond cannot be created. The evil alcohol distribution company (hedge fund) lent the money to the builder (Goldman Sachs) for the construction of the house (the MBS) under the condition that the distribution company could specify to the builder how to build the house (what mortgages would be bundled into the bond).

Let's see: wood and cardboard construction, flammable materials in the walls, gas-lamp lighting, open-fire heating, and—what else would be good?—no smoke or fire alarms and no sprinkler system. That ought to do it! Once the restaurant owner buys the doomed house, the alcohol distribution company can help the process along by (1) insuring the house over and over and over again (buying the CDSs), and (2) selling the house at a low price (shorting the stock).

This is what the SEC charged that Goldman Sachs did; it created MBS bonds that were doomed to fail in order to bet against them. Magnetar Capital routinely demanded that the mortgages being bundled into the MBS bonds by companies like Goldman Sachs and Morgan Stanley be the worst and riskiest or it wouldn't buy the equity tranche.

Why would they bet against their own position? Why would they create bonds that were doomed to default? Because they would make ten times more by betting against the MBS, by purchasing the CDSs, than they would lose on the initial investment in the bond's equity.

It was just too bad if you were the one who bought the house (Iceland) or, in AIG's case, the one who insured the house by selling the CDSs on the bonds. And it was just your bad luck if you were a taxpayer who paid one hundred cents on the dollar to Goldman Sachs for worthless and possibly fraudulent credit default swaps. Had the government nationalized this poison and only paid twenty cents on the dollar, or only paid if the CDS was associated with an actual bond position, the bad guys wouldn't have gotten rich while they blasted the global financial system into dust.

On January 29, 2009, at the height of the crash, the government was considering barring the purchase of credit default swaps by anyone *not* associated with the underlying mortgage-backed security. I wrote in my trading log, "Man, I should hope so." These instruments were what caused the worst of the crisis; they still may have value as insurance, although from my vantage point I'm not even sure of that.

A final note is worthy of mention here. In August 2012 the government dropped the case against Goldman Sachs, citing insufficient evidence to proceed.

Chapter 11

Politics

Who is John Galt?

In 2011, after thirty years of infighting and $20 million spent on production over eighteen years, the first part of a planned trilogy of Ayn Rand's groundbreaking political and science fiction doorstop of a book, *Atlas Shrugged*, was made into a film of the same name. Produced by John Aglialoro and Harmon Kaslow and directed by Paul Johansson, who got the job just nine days before filming was to begin, the first of the three parts stars Taylor Schilling as Dagny Taggart and Grant Bowler as Hank Rearden. A host of of talented, if slightly unfamiliar performers fill out Rand's gigantic cast of characters. Armin

Shimerman, a favorite Star Trek alien of mine, plays Dr. Potter, but without his Ferengi makeup.

When the movie's central character, John Galt, is asked who he is he answers with the guiding theme of the movie and of Ayn Rand's work, "Someone who knows what it's like to work for himself and not let others feed off the profits of his energy."

***

Rand's work was infused with her objectivist philosophy that was born during her family's flight from the Russian Revolution of 1917 and nurtured by her utter hatred of anything remotely socialist. She developed a dedicated following during the Red Scare days of the 1950s. The simple concept that everyone deserves the fruit of one's own effort is undeniably attractive.

I have read all of Rand's books, even the lesser known of them. When I was in college and during my early career as a chemist and engineer, Rand was a staple of draft-beer-lubricated political discussion, although the discussions were universally one-sided in agreement with Rand's concept of rational self-interest. We were the stars, the leaders, the future drivers of human progress. We had triumphed in science, math, athletics, and schoolyard politics; we were not equal to the rest, we were better. We needed our freedom to succeed. It was not fair that the less equal would want to profit from our intellectual efforts or our physical toil—this was obvious to our young and self-centered minds. Yes, it was easy for me to love *Atlas Shrugged*, but then I also loved Robert Heinlein's patriotic vision of a militarist state too. The 1997 movie *Starship Troopers*, directed by Paul Verhoeven, is the film version of Heinlein's novel of the same name. The movie stars Casper Van Dien as Johnny Rico and Denise Richards as Carmen Ibanez. In the movie's near-fascist world of the future, everyone is wealthy and comfortable, but citizenship is reserved for military veterans.

But nothing is ever as simple, or black and white, as we think when we are young; or as simplistic as Ayn Rand believed it to be. America is not the horrifying world of the USSR immediately following the 1917 revolution. It is not the cold and hungry, powerless and senseless world she fled. America is a nation, I fear, where thousands of Dagny Taggarts, Hank Reardens, and John Galts are sentenced to lives that waste their potential, lives driving taxis and flipping hamburgers, because they and their families lack the capital to pay for education. But worse than that fear is my terror that our nation is being led by a dynastic elite that elevates crowds of incompetents like Dr. Potter and Wesley Mouch simply because their families can afford to send them to the best colleges. In *Atlas Shrugged*, the evil Wesley Mouch is played by the wonderful character actor Michael Lerner and Dagny's less-than-worthless brother, James, is played by Matthew Marsden. Recently I watched some conservative commentators on Fox News arguing *against* the need for everyone to have a higher education. I wondered how many of them would not send their own children to college.

The dark world Rand constructed, where the speed of trains and the number of cars in them is limited by some wrongheaded desire to equalize "unfair" competition is horrifying. That kind of social and economic planning *is* what destroyed the Soviet Union and *is* what we need to fight here in America. But it is just as deadly for America if we permit the elimination of competition in our universities, and in our politics, by allowing economic hurdles to prevent our best and brightest from competing. That would be a throwback to the old days of the modern Olympics, when only the affluent had the means to compete, as depicted in the 1981 movie *Chariots of Fire*, a film that was nominated for seven Academy Awards and won four, including best picture. Directed by Hugh Hudson and starring Ben Cross as Harold Abrahams and Ian Charleson as Eric Liddell, the movie is the true story of the 1924 Olympics and exposes the motivations of race and religion in the games, but it also shows the games to have been a rich man's pastime.

During the thirty-five years I have traded the stock and options markets, I have made it my business to invest without the emotions of politics. I have told many of my friends and partners, "I don't care who is in the White House or which party controls Congress; as long as the policies of the party in power are clear, they will be tradable. I can make money." The flea can't affect politics, but he can't ignore them either.

Never before, it seemed to me, had American politics been as rabid and as important as they were as I finished this book in the summer of 2012. When I reread the manuscript from the start, I noticed that the tone of my prose and the strength of my opinions gradually changed as the book progressed. I began writing this book, as part of my trading log, in October 2007, just as the market rolled over, and I continued to write during the long, depressing crash of our markets through 2008, the huge bounce off the March 2009 low, and right on to the time I began editing my log into a readable book in 2012. When I began the project I was still a type A businessperson who saw much of the world in black-and-white terms, but as the project progressed my level of uncertainty rose and my politics evolved.

In my companion book *The Stock Market Flea: Trading the Crash of 2008* I have provided a timeline of those years, showing how American politics affected my trading and my profits, and how my personal beliefs changed to fit the realities of our times. Much of what I included in that book was taken directly from my market newsletter, which I began by warning my immediate friends and family how desperate the times had become and advising them on how to protect themselves from the biggest risks at the height of the crash. Some of it is highly opinionated due to the volatile environment in which it was written.

I'm just a bumpkin from Barstow—worse, I'm a desert rat from thirty-five miles outside of Barstow in a direction that was not on one of the major freeways that pass through the vast Mojave Desert. I don't know anything about anything, as they say. But when I watch our congressional representatives on TV, I am stunned by their stupidity—both Democrats and Republicans. Maybe it is a case of IQ versus the so-called emotional IQ, the kind of intelligence that enables a person with a lot of it to persuade, even take advantage of, other people. Maybe it takes that kind of intelligence to be elected to public office. It is the same kind of intelligence that allows a salesman to be successful. I was a salesman for almost twenty-five years and I did it well, but it never came easily to me. I was lucky in that we sold engineering and chemistry; in this kind of sales the regular kind of IQ can just barely get you through.

In late 2008, when the House of Representatives ideologically voted down the Bush administration's request for the first bank bailout package, TARP, the stock market dropped almost one thousand points. I knew then that we were in for serious trouble—1929 trouble. The year 2008 had been a year of massive declines in the stock and bond markets, but it had proceeded in slow motion, in a seemingly stable way. But this was different, panic was in the air. I called my family members and some close friends that night. Here is a list of recommendations I gave them:

1. Don't own any stocks.

2. Go to the bank and get some cash—enough for a week or two. If the government calls a bank holiday due to a run on the banks, it will be too late to get cash and the bank card system may not function.

3. Go to your warehouse store and fatten up your earthquake kit with water and canned goods. If the financial system collapses, the stores will quickly empty.

4. Fill the tank on your car and keep it full. Gas stations will quickly run out.

5. If you have a gun, get it out and get it ready.

I know it seems odd now, but remember that at about that time, House and Senate leaders met in secret to discuss the imposition of martial law. These were really terrifying days. If the House had not come to its senses, things would have continued on the downward trajectory. But maybe what we see in Congress is not just the absence of smarts; maybe these few to whom we have surrendered our power have more sinister and selfish motives. In *Atlas Shrugged* an intellectual elite deliberately crashes the economy in order to step back in to take power.

In the 1939 movie *Mr. Smith Goes to Washington,* another great flick directed by Frank Capra, James Stewart plays Jefferson Smith, the head of the Boy Rangers. He is appointed to the US Senate despite his boy scout personality because the boss of his state's political machine believes he can be manipulated. When corrupt politicians in Washington scheme to build a dam where Smith wants to build a national boys' camp, Smith launches a filibuster—the old kind where he has to stand up and talk the entire time—not like today, when they just kill the bill without a fight so the majority can't accomplish anything. When the political machine frames Smith for some fabricated wrongdoing and he is about to be run out of the Senate, Smith says, "A certain man in my state wanted to put through this dam for his own profit…came down here and offered me a seat in this Senate for the next twenty years if I voted for a dam that he knew and I knew was a fraud. But I dared to open my mouth against that dam and he promised to break me in two."

Some things never change, or if they do, they just get worse.

Our congressional representatives must have huge emotional IQs. They seem to be able to say and do things that would embarrass regular folks. If history is any measure, they lie and cheat and trade on inside information and take the high ground while molesting congressional pages. They do what is good for them and don't bother themselves with the good of the American people.

Something has got to change.

I have a good friend who is an archconservative. I am what they used to call a Rockefeller Republican: a fiscal conservative and a social progressive. My friend and I frequently have spirited debates about our contrary political views; we also have many business partnerships together. If only our politicians could work together as well.

Recently my partner's son graduated from the University of California–Berkeley and announced that he was a communist. This broke my friend's heart, but I thought it was hilarious. My friend would like his son to go to law school, but the young communist only wants to be an activist and possibly a writer. Law school sounds to me like a great way to actually make a difference, so I was on the dad's side on this one.

The son and I have similar views on many of the excesses of government and corporations. We met for a beer and had a great conversation. It is wonderful to be around young people fresh out of college; their minds are so strong and clear, regardless of their inexperience and optimism. He really thinks he is a communist, and he can defend his position.

I told him that I thought Karl Marx had had some very insightful views on economics, but that he was from a different time. He really didn't understand how a democracy would alter the basic principles on which he based his theories. He thought that the ultimate outcome of unfettered capitalism was an inevitable violent revolution on the part of the masses. He had no concept of how a modern democracy could simply "throw the bums out" in the next election. I also said that I believed we needed to keep the part of capitalism that allows a person to get rich. Up at Berkeley my pal's son learned the failed philosophy, "From each according to their abilities, to each according to their needs." But it is a fact that people work harder when the product of their work goes into their own pocket. Just look at the tremendous economic power unleashed in China after they embraced the concept of personal wealth. Sure we need to take care of our old and our sick, our poor and our weak, our crazy and our dull, but we need enough capitalism to let people get rich.

In China they think they are communists, but they have capitalism coded into their DNA. The amazing rise of China as an economic dynamo started when the Chinese government stopped micromanaging the economy and let individuals succeed. While traveling in China during my first trip in 1992, I noticed that the country was heavy with the bounty of the land—this conflicted confusingly with my memory of my mother's favorite line to get me to eat my vegetables: "There are starving millions in China who would love to have that cauliflower." By the time of my first visit, the Chinese government had given individual farmers tiny plots of land, barely larger than the area of an average American garage, and allowed them to sell the produce they grew and keep the money for themselves. I watched one old guy tilling his tiny garden with a sharpened stick and realized that he and millions like him were the reason the larder was full.

To people such as Alan Tonelson, who advocate the use of trade tariffs in an economic war on China, I respond that the Chinese have very long memories. When I remind my American friends that Hong Kong was stolen from China by the British Empire to use as a base for the illegal importation of opium into China, I get every response from "that's not true" to "you are crazy." But I assure you that the Chinese remember the Opium War. Trade policy? I ask those who recommend a trade war to gain a level playing field with China, "How would we react if another country forced the United States to import heroin? Or if a group of powerful nations divided up New York City for themselves—as was done to Shanghai—and called them *franchises*?" We need to be very, very careful about starting a trade war with our largest trading partner and our biggest creditor, especially one with such a long memory.

When I think about the success of China, a communist country, and Rand's libertarian, rational self-interest, I can't help but remember the way I was compensated as a salesperson. There may be a middle ground here after all. At Betz Laboratories each salesperson chose the ratio of salary to commission. At 80 percent salary and 20 percent commission you were safe and secure, but if you did something great, you wouldn't earn much of a windfall. But if you had confidence in your abilities and believed you were going to do a great job, you might select a compensation plan that was based upon 20 percent salary and 80 percent commission. If you trusted that you would do your job well, and you put in the extra time and effort to do so, you could make a huge difference in the amount you earned. The incentive makes the most competent work harder. It's a pretty good system.

So the pay plan you chose allowed you to be protected, or you could take a risk on yourself and, if you succeeded, you could get rich. In Friedrich Nietzsche's terms, you selected whether you were a master or a slave when you selected your pay plan. I always went for the maximum commission permitted. In a successful society the individual's compensation is tied to the individual's production—in dollar terms to keep it fair, no Japanese-style goals to be met before you get your money. Goals based on metrics not directly related to the individual's economic product—dress code, haircut, outside interests—are simply economic blackmail to force social behaviors the corporation desires, regardless of the individual's bottom-line performance.

Whether or not we believe it to be a good thing, human beings, like the stock market, are motivated by hope and fear. This is the human condition; to ignore it is a huge mistake. The hopes and fears of small business owners will motivate them to work seventy or eighty hours a week in order to achieve the American dream. The idea that someone will do the same out of political fervor is simply false. Look to the failed Soviet Union for evidence of this. In a capitalist system, the individual's opportunity to better his or her life, no matter how remote the possibility, is the foundation of a strong macroeconomy.

Greed and avarice are the foundation of capitalism. The capitalist system takes advantage of these base human drives to extract the most productivity from human efforts. No form of coercion or fear can cultivate the commitment that greed and avarice can generate. It is the fundamental truism of the success of our system. The greedy, especially in the form of corporations, have enough freedom to fuel the growth of our system. We, the citizens, must keep a wary eye on the degree to which the mechanisms used by the greedy penetrate into the critical internal workings of our economy. We must set the beast free, but we must also stand by with the tranquilizer gun.

In America we have legislated control over almost everything. We have laws that control how fast we drive; force us to wear seatbelts and motorcycle helmets; limit the age at which we can drink, smoke, or vote; and designate when and where we can buy and use guns. We do this because we desire to protect ourselves from inherently dangerous situations, not to mention the huge influence of special-interest lobby groups like the insurance companies. When the global risks presented by the banking system are considered, why is it un-American to want to limit the risk-taking of the banks? When things go right, those risks can make the banks lots of money; but when things go poorly, they can cost the country and the people the economic structure needed to be prosperous and safe.

In Alex Proyas's 2004 movie *I, Robot*, Will Smith's character Del Spooner tells Bridget Moynahan's character Susan Calvin, "You are the dumbest smart person I have ever met." This description may be applied to many of the people I just don't understand. For instance, stock market investors, indeed the floor traders at the New York Stock Exchange, are overwhelmingly Republican in spite of the *fact* that the stock market historically does much better under Democratic administrations.

As I have mentioned, I am a social progressive and a fiscal conservative; but when it comes to money and investing I am an apolitical pragmatist, which means—as I have learned over my thirty years of trading—that if I really want to make money I need to temper or change my personal opinions when they conflict with the facts. When Treasury bond interest rates hit historic lows, Larry Summers, ranking monetary advisor to the administration of president Barack Obama and past secretary of the Treasury, advised that we borrow more now, when it is free money. The Cato Institute and other smart organizations and experts exploded with anger. But why? They would refinance their own homes at a lower rate, wouldn't they? A Cato spokesman said, "The money is not free, we will eventually need to pay it back." But would we? The principal will be devalued away at normal inflation rates in just a few years, and I believe we are in for a period of elevated inflation rates in the not-too-distant future.

If you could refinance your home at a zero percentage rate, would you do it? If so, why? Apply that answer to the national question and you have my argument for stimulus policy. In 1936 the country lost its political will to stimulate the economy and raised taxes and cut spending in an ill-advised effort to balance the budget. The result was the transformation of a serious recession into the Great Depression. Don't the folks at Cato have history books? By the middle of 2012 it appeared that we were on the same political path as in 1936, with our heroine in the rowboat (our economy) floating ever faster toward the waterfall—the so-called fiscal cliff.

Modern countries exist on their ability to borrow for the future. The British Empire was born out of almost constant warfare when they were the first nation to borrow the money they needed for war from their new and powerful banking system. Before this financial breakthrough, countries needed to take the time to collect taxes before having the necessary funds to go to war—this delay could mean the difference between victory and defeat. At its zenith, two-thirds of the world's land mass and three-fourths of the world's people fell under the control of the British Empire. At times, governmental borrowing is a "real cool hand" to play.

In late July 2011, as I watched the vaudeville of our leaders tiptoeing along the cliff edge of national default, I was not surprised. This was just more example of what had been inflicted upon the Bush administration when it needed Congress to pass TARP in order to bail out the banking industry. The country, and in fact the entire world, was waiting for the US Congress to step up to the plate and allocate funds to pay our bills. The posturing of both political parties reminded me of the judgment of Solomon—and America was the baby.

In the Old Testament story, two women come to King Solomon with a baby. Both women claim to be the baby's mother. The wise king brings out a sword and tells them he will cut the baby in two and give each half. The false mother says, "OK, cut away," but the true mother cries out and tells the king to give the baby to the other woman. The king realizes that she is the true mother and gives the baby to her.

There is a political bloc in the US House of Representatives that would not vote for an increase in the debt ceiling under any circumstances—think Michele Bachmann. Cut away! They are willing to crash the plane to avoid going to anywhere Obama wants to go in it.

But hey, the rest of us are on the plane too! Can't we at least land the plane before you fight over the controls?

If Congress had not ultimately raised the debt ceiling in 2011, to pay the bills *they* had run up, we would probably have had economic disaster—the baby would have been cut in two. But we don't have a king, a wise decision maker like Solomon, to decide on things like the debt-ceiling question. The people we elected to Congress needed to do it. When the dust settled, the bills were paid, but the world had lost faith and trust in our government and for the first time in history, the credit rating of the United States was downgraded. This downgrade has already cost us—you and me—billions of dollars more for the interest we pay on our tremendous debt. Where is the economic sense in that?

Alan Greenspan believed for most of his career that any regulation was bad. He believed that the markets were a self-correcting system. If someone defrauded his or her clients, as Bernard Madoff did, the markets would eventually expose him, eliminating the need for regulation. Greenspan believed that the banks would never put themselves in positions that could conceivably cause them to fail because they had their own self-interest to protect. When this proved to be false and the banking system almost collapsed, Greenspan told Congress that he had been wrong. Everything he had believed had been a false paradigm. The banks had taken on suicidal positions while the highest-level banking executives had become unbelievably rich. The self-protection instinct did not protect the banks, but it did protect the executives.

Everything John Maynard Keynes said about the economy and the markets has been proved correct—*twice*, in the 1930s and today. Everything Milton Friedman and the Chicago school of economics believed has been proved wrong—*twice*. It is almost impossible to understand how intelligent people can look at history and ignore the facts. The markets are emotional and *not* rational and they need to be regulated.

One of my most conservative friends put it this way: "It is against the will of God, religion, and common decency to kill another human being, but we still have a law against it—and a jail to put the killer inside."

The Friedman disciples would have us cut all stimulus spending to reduce the deficit. Yes, eventually reducing spending is critical to getting our economy back on track; spending is the part of the equation we can control. As an individual works to earn income, the country needs to collect taxes, but both have less control over the income than the outlays. If we run the country *not* like a business but like a family, we could get things back under control. Sure, we can sharpen our skills, go back to school, or get a second job, but the impact on income is slow, if effective at all. But the outlays, our spending, can be changed quickly and easily—just as a family does when it has a financial crisis.

But we can't just cut all stimulus spending during a crisis. We need the spending to create some inflation—to "prime the pump," as we have done over and over again since the 1929 crash. The problem with this crisis, when compared to the crash of 1987, when the Federal Reserve provided liquidity that turned the crash around almost immediately, is that the country's balance sheet had already been made too large by the Bush administration, which believed ignorantly that "deficits don't matter." When the time came to borrow and spend, we were already in hock up to our collective neck. Now we need to prevent a deflationary collapse without the borrowing power we had in 1987, and heaven help us if we increase taxes and start a trade war at the same time.

By the middle of 2012, our politicians, Democrats and Republicans, were jockeying for position in preparation for the upcoming elections, ignoring the work of the people that they were hired to do. I wrote that we should surprise them all and vote all the incumbents out. Get rid of all the old stale ideas and bring in all new blood. It could not get any worse.

Right now the ultraright wing of the Republican Party controls only about 10–15 percent of the total votes in only one of three branches of government, the US House of Representatives. But their suicide bomber–like tactics—do exactly as I say or I will blow up the economy—have brought the government to a halt.

In Washington an epic battle rages. Our leaders are at an impasse; there doesn't appear to be any common ground between two opposite ways of thinking. It is difficult to understand how so many intelligent and well-meaning legislators can have such diametrically opposed views on what is good for our country. We call it the budget battle but it represents so much more. The battle represents the fundamental difference in philosophies that has infused American economic debate for over one hundred years: trickle down versus bottom up.

Nietzsche believed that in the human population there are two kinds of people: masters and slaves. The masters are the kind of people who were glorified by Ayn Rand in her novels—the movers and shakers, the drivers of progress, the people who invent new things and operate the machine of industry: the fighters and the strugglers. The slaves are the kind of people who are quietly led through life. They have learned that if they just go along they won't need to struggle or think; others—the masters—will take care of thinking and leading.

Nietzsche believed that all progress came from the small minority of masters leading the unthinking masses of slaves forward. He wrote that only a small minority of the human population actually deserved to live; the vast majority, the slaves, only had value as workers or soldiers in efforts managed by the masters.

In Ridley Scott's 1982 classic science fiction movie, *Blade Runner*, a subclass of humans is genetically engineered to be used as soldiers and prostitutes. The manufactured and subjugated humans are superior in every measurable way save their genetically engineered five-year life-spans. In the climactic rooftop scene near the end of the film, Rutger Hauer's character Roy, the last of a group of these new beings confronts the blade runner, Deckard (Harrison Ford), who has murdered—"retired"—the rest. Standing over the cowering Deckard, Roy says, "Quite an experience to live in fear, isn't it? That's what it is to be a slave." Who has the right to make a slave of another human being? What makes some believe they are more deserving of the right to lead, to be the master?

In the book *Tarzan of the Apes*, Edgar Rice Burroughs postulated what would happen to a boy of "good breeding" if he were dropped as an infant into the wilderness. Burroughs said that breeding would win out and the boy would become a master regardless of his lack of family, schooling, or religious training. Blood—genetics to us—was the deciding factor. The other side of this coin is that a slave, regardless of the resources available, will always be a slave, a drag on society. The natural order of things, according to Nietzsche, is that the most gifted should rule the less gifted in a master-slave relationship. The slaves are resources for the masters to use in their quest for progress. Eventually, from the ranks of the masters, the ultimate fulfillment of mankind will be the evolution of the *Übermensch*, or superman. The *Übermensch* will rule the world with only his ideal of progress restraining his power over humanity.

Nietzsche thought that Western Judeo-Christian morals were developed during the time that the Jews were slaves in Egypt. As slaves, it was best if the Jews were subservient and obedient: the less resistance they showed to the pharaoh, the less trouble they got in return. Turning the other cheek is a good thing for a slave to learn to do. After all, the meek will inherit the earth; all the slaves needed to do was wait.

Nietzsche believed that this ancient experience of slavery created the Judeo-Christian moral structure that guides the actions of our lives and of our nation today. He believed that Judeo-Christian morals, with the philosophy of love and forgiveness, of peace and generosity, of obedience to God and religion, of equality in the eyes of God are an impediment to the development of mankind as a species. He believed that this slave mind-set did nothing to further the development of the species and that all progress depended on the few masters born among us. The natural order of things was for the masters to use their superior intellect, talent, and strength to dominate the slaves, leading civilization forward in the process. The theory leads to the conclusion that if the species of humankind is to develop, and if human civilization is to progress, the masters must dominate the slaves in order to drive societal evolution forward.

In Nietzsche's mind, the battle lines were drawn: the humanistic, caring, unselfish philosophy of Western Old Testament–based religions versus the realistic, objective, cynical philosophy typified by the idea that the survival of the fittest is the natural order of the world. If slaves are willing to turn the other cheek, masters need to be willing to slap them twice. He believed, contrary to the Judeo-Christian moral fabric, that the masters should not fight their natural instincts to dominate their weaker brethren; this dominance is the only way to evolve the species and further civilization.

Today in Washington we have two groups of legislators. On one hand we have the Republicans, who believe the best thing for America is to deconstruct the New Deal. They honestly believe that the best thing for America is to let the most gifted individuals take all that they can grab because this drives progress forward and the less gifted will benefit from an overall increase in the wealth of the nation. They say, "Don't tax the rich because these are the people who invest their riches and create the jobs." A general increase in wealth will allow some to trickle down to the less gifted, improving their lives. The other group in Washington, the Democrats, believes that all men are equal and deserve a level playing field in life—even if this requires the government to give them an added, some say unfair, advantage over the more gifted. They honestly believe that providing for the poor and helpless is the moral responsibility of the nation, even if this means taking resources from the rich and powerful and "redistributing" them to the poor and weak.

We must accept that some are more gifted than others—anyone who has played high school athletics can testify to that—and it appears that the best way to motivate the gifted is by allowing them to keep the fruits of their labors. So any economically successful system must accept and utilize this truism. But what about the less fortunate? What is the responsibility of the master class?

In Rand's novel *Atlas Shrugged*, a group of discontented masters drops out of society and holes up in a secret mountain site. Hidden under a force-field dome that also makes them invisible, their superior strength, intelligence, and abilities power the creation of new technologies and weapons that will allow them to regain their rule over the chaos of slave self-rule. The masters, using no force, simply allow the economic structure of society to completely collapse so they can step back in to take over. Is this what the ultraright wing of the Republican Party wants? Does it think it needs to force the government into default as part of the path to its way of doing things? If so, these people are dangerous.

There is a master-and-slave society in America today. The Fundamentalist Church of Latter Day Saints (FLDS) is an ultraorthodox sect with a single prophet (leader), Warren Jeffs, who rules his cult from within a tight group of older men who get the most benefit from the cult. The younger men are tossed out into the world and the young girls, as young as ten or twelve, are forced into polygamous marriages with the older men. We consider their culture to be amoral and have arrested Jeffs, the cult's leader. But the cult exemplifies Nietzsche's natural state:

a few more powerful, possibly more gifted, individuals have taken all the culture's riches, including the bodies of the faithful, as their private property. Is this really the kind of society we want to have?

In a study done to evaluate why some people survive disasters while others do not, researchers interviewed many people who had lived through deadly accidents. One of the most interesting examples was of a fire on a plane as it sat on the tarmac. One lady, who was sitting four rows away from an exit, lived through the fire, while others sitting much closer to the exit died. The difference, the researchers found, was a drive to live that trumped any societal values of right and wrong. The lady climbed up onto the heads and shoulders of the other passengers and clawed her way to the front, crawling over them to get to the exit first. The researchers stated that this is a common thread among survivors—self-preservation with no compunction regarding the deaths of others. Survivors selfishly save themselves even if this costs the lives of others. This basest of survival instincts seems very similar to the philosophy that only the most gifted deserve life and that the sacrifice of the less gifted is a necessary unpleasantness. Are these the instincts we want to institutionalize in our government?

I have a friend who could be a hero in an objectivist Ayn Rand novel. From nothing she used her strength and intelligence to forge a good life for herself and her daughter. Pregnant at sixteen, she was forced into life early and alone. When her daughter was born, it was discovered that she was a quadriplegic. My friend, in the mold of a Rand superhero, buckled down, and with her own abilities conquered her world. She put herself through nursing school while supporting a household and providing the unending care her daughter required. Now she is an independent woman with the worst of her life behind her. She manages a maternity ward in a local hospital, drives a new car, and owns her own home. Her daughter has a fulfilling life online with her social media friends and a job as a translator. My friend is the kind of person Nietzsche would have called a master.

One day while hiking in the local hills, my friend and I had the opportunity for a long conversation on the plight of America. She told me about the young, unproductive women who come to her hospital and repeatedly have children out of wedlock. These women have no means of support and depend on the government for financial aid and medical care. Many of these mothers, my friend says, are not legal residents of the United States and come to America to have their babies as a method of gaining legal status here. She said that if she were in charge, these women would be *forcibly sterilized.*

My surprised response was to agree that these mothers are gaming the system, but that I have serious issues with giving the government the right to select who has the right to reproduce or to live. I told her that it had been tried before and that it had resulted in the genocide of millions during World War II. Once a government has the power to decide which of its citizens deserves to live, which ones are productive members of society, and which ones only consume resources, the nation steps closer to the slippery slope of eugenics. I asked her if she realized that her daughter would be at the top of the list for extermination in that terrifying world. She couldn't make the connection.

So this is the question: Do we want to impede the economic progress of the species by taking care of our old, our sick, our frail, our dim? Or do we want to drive economic progress forward without concern for the less fortunate? These are questions for all of us to consider. What does each of us want from our government? But we must be very careful about what we think we want. As the old saying goes, "Be careful what you wish for, you might just get it."

Right now there is a huge debate about how much we want to spend on government, and at the same time we debate the undesirability of raising taxes. But these are secondary questions; the important issue is who we want to be. We, as a nation, need to resolve the most basic question of what kind of country we want to have. We need to back off the *how much* and evaluate the *what.*

The American Dream and Taxes

Some people think that the American dream is home ownership, but that is not correct. The American dream is crossing the wide ocean in steerage with only a few extra cents in your pockets, disembarking at Ellis Island with tens of thousands of others, finding work, any work—more work and long hours turning into long years—and finally waking up one day to find that you are wealthy. That is the American dream: work hard and you too can be one of the "1 percent."

The class warfare debate coloring the presidential election politics is a red herring. The question isn't how much wealth the wealthy have or how little the poor have; the question is whether the American dream is still sound. I don't think so. The game has been fixed in such a way that essentially bars the poor from attaining wealth. Unless the poverty-level individual has legs like Betty Grable, or an arm like Sandy Koufax, or a brain like Steve Jobs, no amount of work will raise this person's station in life because the work he or she is forced to do is the wrong kind of work.

Like the people in Bangladesh who needed to eat the seed grain sent to them during the 1974 famine, the poor work long hours at meaningless and unfulfilling jobs and are too exhausted to do anything that could further their dreams. I'm not saying that occasionally a Steve Jobs won't blow through the barriers in place to protect the status quo, but these people are exceptional and rare. That kind of game-changing ability will succeed just as well in a balanced system, with rules and a level playing field, as they will in a system manufactured over centuries to protect the privilege of people whose only genius is that of birth and whose only talent is their vast wealth.

I understand where the Tea Party is coming from, I really do. Another of their literary favorites is the classic 1949 novel by George Orwell, *1984*. I read it in high school and it scared the hell out of me. When I watched the 1956 movie version, with the hopelessness and powerlessness of citizens dominated by a totalitarian state made even more frightening by the black-and-white cinematography, I was even more terrified. Directed by Michael Anderson, *1984* starred Edmond

O'Brien as the downtrodden Winston Smith and Jan Sterling as Julia. When trying to explain why she had betrayed him, Julia tells Winston, "Sometimes they threaten you with something—something you can't stand up to, can't even think about. And then you say, 'Don't do it to me, do it to someone else, do it to so-and-so.'" It is enough to make anyone want to buy some guns and ammunition.

Then in the real 1980s, with American industry down on the mat, new ways of doing business came out of the seemingly invincible Japanese *keiretsu* conglomerates—philosophies that ran counter to everything that made us Americans. The Japanese team mind-set, with everything done for the good of the corporation, robbed American workers of what had made them the best in the world: creativity and independence. It became undesirable to be a "rugged individualist." These Orwellian business practices penetrated American industry, resulting in US workers being forced to wear the personality-killing overalls of the team that looked menacingly like those in Anderson's dark film. I was as afraid that Orwell's vision had come to pass as any Tea Party member. Yes, we need to be on guard against the powers of the state.

The objectivist philosophy of Ayn Rand, as stimulated by the philosophy of Freidrich Nietzsche, is a core belief of the old America, the America of the rugged individualist. It is also a basic tenet of the new Tea Party. But uncontrolled, in a modern world, these beliefs can be as damaging as the ego-stealing philosophies of the 1980s. We need to temper these ideas and guard against the excesses of self-interest just as vigilantly.

If the Friedman free-market chauvinists believe so fervently in business and market Darwinism, why are they so adamantly against what they have derogatorily tagged the "death tax"? The inheritance tax only applies to the very, very rich. The estate tax exemption for 2012 is $5.12 million, up from $5 million for calendar year 2011. The amount a person is permitted to receive—$5.12 million before a cent of tax is paid—is actually going up during the "liberal" Obama presidency.

So, potentially, a person who has no exceptional abilities save for the luck of birth; no special talent, strength, or art; no extraordinary intellect earned through tens of millennia of natural selection; nothing that would provide a evolutionary reproductive advantage—that is, a person who could be the daughter of a wealthy hotel magnate but otherwise a bimbo could begin life with the gigantic advantage of $5 million tax free. Where is the Darwinism in that? I do not think that a person should be born into wealth and privilege; wealth and privilege need to be earned in each generation to avoid the creation of a nobility class and the inefficiency of the incompetent made powerful by birth.

But the real problem is the belief system of the poor. They still believe in the American dream—the real one, not the home ownership lie—and this causes them to act, to vote against their own interests. Why would $50,000-a-year blue-collar workers ever worry about the inheritance tax? Because they have been conned into thinking they have a chance to someday actually have the $5 million. They have again been tricked into letting their own greed protect the rich.

When I'm letting the water run down the drain to let it warm up, I feel guilty about the waste. I need to resist thinking, "Hey, I saved the world over seven million gallons of water every day with my reclaimed-water project in Hawaii. I'm still seven million gallons ahead of what I'm wasting every day." Maybe this is the attitude of the ultrarich. The wealthy may chose to take smart risks and by doing so make big profits, and as a result pay huge amounts of taxes because they are making lots and lots of money. They may well feel that they took the risk so they should keep the money. Why should they pay tax at a higher rate when they have taken higher risks? Good question.

The tax code need not be regressive. Yes, people making more should pay more, but not at a higher percentage rate. We just need to get rid of the deductions to make things fair. The flat tax favored by the conservatives could work, as long as it is just and does not shift the burden to the middle class. I heard one TV pundit say angrily, "The liberals want to do away with the loopholes the rich use to avoid paying taxes, but then they want to keep the money." Well of course!

The other side of a flat tax – say 30 percent tax rate for all – is that everyone keeps 70 percent of his or her income. Sure, 70 percent of a $10 million investment profit is a lot more, in dollar terms, than 70 percent of a $50,000-a-year blue-collar job, but it is the same percentage. The blue-collar guy is left with $35,000, which he may need to support a family. The wealthy guy is left with $7 million of profit to do with as he sees fit. On the surface it may seem unfair to the blue-collar guy that the millionaire gets to keep so much, but why should the wealthy guy pay taxes at a higher percentage rate? Yes he has put $7 million in his pocket, but he has paid $3 million in taxes! It is the system of loopholes and special deductions that allows him to pay much less than his fair share.

I believe the wealthy and the poor should pay tax at the same percentage rate. The wealthy should not be able to game the tax code and pay 14 percent while the blue-collar guy pays 30 percent, but at the same time I don't believe the wealthy should pay 40 percent, or 50 percent or more, just because they made more. Fair share means "fair" share, not higher share. If anything, a graduated tax code should go the opposite way the Democrats would like. At some point the person paying a huge tax bill should get a discount, not a penalty, for doing so. A productivity discount, if you will.

During the last twenty-five years, but especially during the last dozen years, we have witnessed the biggest redistribution of wealth since the robber barons of the nineteenth century; by some measures, the redistribution of recent years has been even larger. Alan Dunn in *Forbes*, not known for its liberal tendencies, says the rich have grown much wealthier while the poor have grown poorer. "The fact is," he says, "that the upper classes really are taking money from the poor..."

Nobel Laureate Joseph Stiglitz says the richest 1 percent of the population now holds over 40 percent of the country's wealth. The estimate of how much they held in 1970 was about 20 percent of the wealth.

The richest 5 percent now owns over 68 percent of the wealth. Under our current structure, the fear that tax rates will be used to redistribute wealth is unfounded. I wouldn't worry about the wealthy; they work very hard to avoid paying taxes, whatever the tax rates may be. They have tax lawyers, accountants, dummy corporations, tax-exempt charitable enterprises, offshore accounts—you name it, they will use it to avoid paying taxes.

The hugely wealthy—and as Gordon Gekko said in the movie *Wall Street*, "I don't mean some $250,000-a-year stockbroker, I mean really liquid," are not concerned about normal income taxes—they don't work for a living, they invest. They do fear the capital gains tax, as this reduces the yield they make on their capital. But there is no free lunch—the government will get its money one way or the other; either it gets the money through taxes, or it will borrow it. Without taxes to pay down the debt the government will let runaway inflation devalue the money it has borrowed so it can pay back the debt a few pennies on the dollar.

It is informative to evaluate how the ultrawealthy, and the politically powerful, are affected by inflation, a hidden tax, as compared to the capital gains tax. If a really rich person makes $5 million per year in capital gains on a net worth of $100 million, and assuming his accountants have not worked their magic, the rich person would pay $750,000 in taxes at the current 15 percent capital gains tax rate—$1.25 million in taxes at a higher 25 percent rate. Outrageous amounts! But after they have bought five or ten big houses and some yachts and cool cars, they can't buy many more big ticket items. This means after a year or two of crazy buying, they start to save most of what they make. So even at the 25 percent rate, they would pay about $1.25 million in taxes and save about $3.75 million. Their net wealth goes up about 4 percent. Oh boy, a higher base for investment gains next year!

Compare this to the oil worker who makes $50,000 per year in taxable wages. He pays about 25 percent income tax, or $12,500 per year—it's really much more, but for ease of comparison I'll use this—leaving him $37,500 to spend. Well, with rent on a house and a family to feed and gas to get to work, the $38K doesn't go very far. Since our oil worker spends all he makes, you can deduct another 5–8 percent for sales tax the rich saver won't pay. He can't save a thing—so much for Horatio Alger. Remember that since the wealthy don't work, they don't pay income tax, Social Security tax, or Medicare tax. They don't pay for Social Security or Medicare, so they won't get it. Is it any wonder why they want to abolish these programs?

It is much more profitable for a wealthy person to pay 15 percent capital gains and let inflation run wild. Since the wealthy don't buy much, in terms of a percentage of their income, and since they can keep up with inflation within their savings with high-yield investments, inflation doesn't have a huge impact on them, except maybe that all of their houses appreciate in value. But the oil worker has got a problem. He doesn't pay capital gains because he doesn't have any capital. But he does pay the hidden inflation tax. He spends 100 percent of his income. With an inflation rate of 5 percent, his buying power is reduced to less than $28,000 in five years. This inflation rate sounds big now, but this is tiny compared to what happened during the 1970s. The oil worker needs a 7 percent raise every year just to keep up. Eventually he won't be able to pay his bills.

Although my big-picture view of high inflation has not developed by the fall of 2013, I still believe we are in for a long hard period of high inflation once it begins. This will be fine for the very wealthy, especially if the capital gains tax is kept at 15 percent, but our oil worker is screwed. Every year the wealthy person will be able to save more and more and the oil worker will be able to buy less and less. This is true even if the capital gains tax rate were 50 percent or 70 percent or more.

There has also been much said during the last few years about communism and Karl Marx. Marx believed that the inevitable end to unfettered capitalism would be the concentration of all the wealth into the hands of a few wealthy and powerful people—the plutocracy. Marx believed that the wealthy and powerful would naturally use their wealth and power to gain ever more wealth and power and that the unavoidable end result would be violent revolution, ending in the overthrow of the plutocracy by the weak and poor. Off with their heads!

The reason Marx and all the communist states that rose and fell in the twentieth century were all wrong was that they couldn't comprehend the workings of a truly free and efficient democracy. They couldn't understand what it meant to be able to vote out the guys with whom you don't agree. There's no need for the guillotine in America; just the vote.

Chapter 12

Trading

Buy Low and Sell High

One of the funniest stock-market movies of all time is *Trading Places*, the 1983 update of Mark Twain's *The Prince and the Pauper*. Directed by John Landis, this hilarious comedy starred Dan Aykroyd (as Louis Winthorpe III), Eddie Murphy (as "Billy Ray" Valentine) and Jamie Lee Curtis (as Ophelia). But the show was stolen by Ralph Bellamy and Don Ameche, the rich and evil Duke brothers, who made this movie the crowning touch of their long and distinguished careers. When Louis and Billy Ray are about to corner the frozen orange juice market with inside information they have squeezed (sorry) from the mean but incompetent Clarence Beeks (played by

Paul Gleason), the Duke brothers' hired thug, Louis gives Billy Ray some last minute advice: "Think big, think positive. Never show any sign of weakness. Always go for the throat. Buy low, sell high. Fear... that's the other guy's problem."

That doesn't sound so difficult.

***

I didn't start out wanting to be a day trader, as some young studs did in the late 1990s. I just wanted to buy some stock and have it for a very long time and not think about it. Then, in some nebulous time in the future I would check back in to my account, sell the stock for a huge profit and retire. Well, that strategy didn't work out too well for me—or for millions of others who got caught in the dot-com bubble of the late 1990s, the real estate bubble at the beginning of the new century, and the stock market crash of 2008. Money invested in the Dow 30 or the S&P 500 in 2000 would be flat to lower after more than a decade. A passbook account would have done better over that time.

What the heck? Whatever happened to 10 percent compounded yearly in the stock market?

Every investor has heard of Warren Buffett, the Wizard of Omaha. Buffet adheres to a strict philosophy of value investing. He has become a legend because of the tremendous success of his investments. There is an entire class of investors who do nothing else but try to mimic every move he makes. To paraphrase an old TV commercial of the now defunct Dean Witter Reynolds brokerage company, "When Warren Buffet talks, people listen." Buffet is well known for saying, "Our favorite holding period is forever." The TV pundits often use this quote to argue for the buy-and-hold strategy of investing.

What they don't say is that when Buffett buys into a company, as he did with Goldman Sachs and Bank of America during the 2008 banking crisis, he gets sweetheart deals that get him in at levels much lower than are available to the average person. He begins his investments as a big winner and then gains from there. It's much easier to take a temporary loss when you start out way ahead and are still in the money after the hit.

Hmmm, let's see how forever would have worked for me. Recently I went back into my trading log and dug up some old trades, and then I looked up what the stocks were doing in June 2012. The results were startling.

In the first table below are some equities I traded in the early 1980s and what they traded for in June 2012. For you purists, let me say in advance that the early 1980s were a long time ago, before the widespread use of computerization; there are probably a couple of mistakes I missed in the table due to splits or mergers. The concept is the same.

How About Thirty Years? 1983 to 2012

EQUITY	JUNE 1983	JUNE 2012*
Murphy Oil	$28	$44.22
Louisiana Pacific	$32	$8.54
Symbol Tech	$16	0
Sealed Power	$50	0
Alamco	$5	0
Clinitherm	$5	0
Ultra Systems	$20	0
Fard Robotics	$4	0
Energy Conservation Devices	$37	$0.021
Ferro Fluids	$12	$0.0072
Covington Brothers	$4	0

* Corrected for split or liquidation including takeover

Sure looks like being a trader was a better way to accumulate wealth than being a forever investor. OK, those stock picks came from a time when I was just starting out and they may have been too speculative. What about better, and more recent, stock picks and a shorter forever period?

How About a Dozen Years? 2000 to 2012

EQUITY	1999–2000	JUNE 2012
Amazon	$82	$210.34
Intel	$75	$24.95
IBM	$125	$187.94
eBay	$141	$39.07
Exxon	$80	$77.34
Mobil	$105	0*
Texaco	$67	0*
Chevron	$84	$95.95
Oracle	$42	$26.06
Dell	$46	$11.89
Myriad Genetics	$145	$22.62
Xilinx	$90	$30.84
Altera	$109	$32.07
Compaq Computer	$28	0*
Cabot Microelectronics	$28	$30.15
Cell Pathways	$31	0*
Incyte	$96	$20.40
Millennium Pharmaceuticals	$125	0*
Human Genome	$158	$13.35
Amgen	$72	$68.36
Hercules	$13	$2.96
Verizon	$56	$41.23
Celera	$100	0*
Citigroup	$65	$2.50*
Texas Instruments	$146	$8.65
Exodus Communications	$91	0*

* Corrected for split or liquidation, including takeover.

There are a few notable winners—Amazon and IBM stand out—but on the whole this portfolio would have been a dog to hold for a dozen years. I admit that this is a narrow view of what has transpired over the last fifteen or thirty years, and these were my picks, but the S&P, Dow, and NASDAQ averages performed in very much the same way over the last dozen years. Market pundits call the first decade of the new century "the lost decade" because of this performance. My point is that if you really want to accumulate wealth, you can't believe that "trading" is an evil word, a risky way of managing money. When the fluff is stripped away, trading is simply taking profits when they are there to take.

In 2000, I accepted another engineering sales job. After almost a decade working for Betz outside of North America I was going back to Los Angeles; I had gone over to the enemy's camp to join Nalco Chemical Company, as many of the top people in Betz had done after the Hercules takeover. While living abroad I had been unable to speculate in real estate or trade the stock market. Contrary to the belief of my coworkers, who had stayed home in the United States, it had been almost impossible to accumulate any lasting wealth while working overseas as an expatriate. Yes, the company paid for everything—travel, rent, utilities, car and driver, even taxes—but real wealth accumulation requires hands-on investing and active management. And this is just not possible when you are ten thousand miles away from good real estate deals and the stock market has been closed for half a day when you wake up. Forget about trading options when you travel 60 percent of the time.

After my repatriation I realized I would need to book some pretty solid gains to make up for lost time and build something for my retirement. But the timing could not have been worse; by 2000 the markets had entered a the period of sickening ups and downs that would produce little, if any net growth for almost ten years. The market indexes would wind up at the same or lower levels after ten years of directionless turbulence, and then finally roll off a cliff in 2008. And as the markets collapsed, the myth of deregulation deflated with them; so much for miracle of unbridled markets.

After I got back to Los Angeles, I buckled down and concentrated on my engineering job and on my investments. I made plenty of mistakes, but I did well enough that by the time I was paying my 2006 taxes, in April 2007, I realized that I would have taken home almost the same amount of after-tax income had I not worked a day peddling specialty chemicals to oil refineries.

Really, I'm working this crappy job for free?

After thirty years of investing, working, and saving I found myself in mid-2007 living in a spectacular rented house overlooking Los Angeles Harbor with a view across the bay to Saddleback Mountain in Orange County. I was still working as a chemical engineering consultant, but I was unhappy with the job, my boss, and how I was being treated. I had sold all my real estate and had gone to cash in my retirement and investment accounts, but I was still trading options in what I called my high-frequency trading account.

One day, while I drank a cup of coffee and gazed out through the floor-to-ceiling glass wall of my living room, the *Black Pearl* sailed by just offshore of Cabrillo Beach. I had forgotten about the flyer that had been taped to my front door, notifying me of the upcoming assault on the beach and apologizing for the noise from cannon fire. In 2007 the filming being done just outside my windows was for the next chapter of the Pirates of the Caribbean series, *Pirates of the Caribbean: At World's End*. The *Black Pearl* has been made famous in four Disney films (so far) based upon the theme-park ride of the same name. The movie stars the always entertaining Johnny Depp as Captain Jack Sparrow, Orlando Bloom as Will Turner, and Keira Knightley as Elizabeth Swann. Directed by Gore Verbinski, the filming provided us many days and nights of live entertainment.

While watching the movie-making magic, I realized that for the seven years I had been back in Los Angeles I had not written one word creatively. I had not even kept up with my personal journal, which I had begun in 1978 and had compulsively updated almost every day for thirty years while working and traveling the world. I had written four or five huge pieces of technical writing for customers, including one three-hundred-page report that was best read on computer because of the thousands of links to spreadsheets, laboratory chemical analyses, elemental determinations, and photographs, but I had sacrificed the creative writing that I had loved all my life.

I had become, since my return to Los Angeles, what I liked least about others in the business world: an automaton who lived for work and for the accumulation of wealth, devoid of creativity and art. When I looked at myself, I was surprised and disappointed. Early in my career I could have gone much further in the business community if that had been what I wanted out of life. I had built enough wealth to retire comfortably and I didn't like the work I was doing. It was time for a change.

By this time I had been speaking Mandarin Chinese for ten years, but I couldn't write a character of it. I wanted to learn how to read and write. I moved away from the beach, the first time in twenty-five years that I couldn't see the ocean from where I lived, so I could go back to school. I spent nights and weekends of my last six months as an engineering consultant in the San Gabriel Valley, the real Chinatown east of Los Angeles, attending Mount San Jacinto Community College, studying Chinese and oiling up my creative writing skills, which had long gone rusty while I had concentrated on making money.

But all through 2007 I traded in my high-frequency account. The structure I used during most of the year was to load up on something very conservative—I had the small trading account almost 100 percent in California municipal bonds with high interest rates and no federal or state income tax liabilities. Then I would trade options on margin within the account. Much of the time I wouldn't even have the margin interest charges because if you buy and sell in the same day—the goal for an options trader—you don't pay any margin interest. Life was good; I was making 4–5 percent on the munis and I was using the equity to fund my options trading.

When one of my coworkers asked how my trading was going I told him I felt like Keanu Reeves's character in *The Matrix* when he finally became stronger than the agents. *The Matrix* (1999) is the first film of a trilogy written and directed by Larry and Andy Wachowski. The movies starred Keanu Reeves, Laurence Fishburne, Carrie-Anne Moss, Joe Pantoliano, and Hugo Weaving. Remember the scene where Neo (Keanu Reeves) is fighting the agent in the subway station and he seems amazed at his effortless ability to flick away the agent's punches? That is how I felt. I believed I had figured out the options market. Every trade was making money. I just needed to make the trades bigger to really make a killing. Then, in November 2007, reality came to my door. On one very bad day of trading Goldman Sachs calls I dropped $82,000 at expiration.

Hey, I thought I had this figured out!

What is trading? Is it some wild-eyed gambler throwing money at a roulette wheel? As you might expect, I don't think so. I think trading is acting on your big-picture thesis of where the markets are going, but using every trick you can think of to limit your risk and optimize your profits.

One of the greatest market traders of the twentieth century was Jesse Livermore, whose trading became legend after he shorted the markets in time to catch the 1929 crash. The publication of Edwin Lefèvre's book *Reminiscences of a Stock Operator,* a fictionalized biography of Livermore's trades and thought processes, was first published as a series of stories in the *Saturday Evening Post* between June 1922 and May 1923. Livermore began his career as a ticker reader who watched the tape in what were then called bucket shops—places where you could bet on the movement in stocks but where there were no real stocks to be bought; it reminds me of the derivatives markets today. He was known for being one of the very best ticker readers and repeatedly made fortunes doing it. But as time went by and fortunes won became fortunes lost, Livermore learned that the really big money was in predicting the macrodirections in world economics and thereby the markets. I came across the book when a friend recommended it. He was a young chemical engineer who had suffered a few years under my intense management style before I went overseas. He recommended the book when he learned I had given up engineering to trade for myself.

About the time I was coming back to North America, my young friend had already given up engineering to be a day trader. He was what Jesse Livermore would have called a plunger; he preferred shorting stocks, a taste I have never acquired, and he did it very successfully during the bursting of the dot-com bubble in 2001. Being an avid surfer—odd because he learned it late in life after moving to California from Pennsylvania—he bought a big house with an ocean view in Hermosa Beach with his earnings. A few years later he got married and had some children, which forced him back into the boring and restrictive world of engineering. I lost track of him just as the market broke down in 2008, and I don't know if he was shorting anything during the biggest downturn since Jesse Livermore's time, but I hope he was in the market. The book is must reading for anyone who wants to make money in the stock market, and it is quite entertaining.

I don't think the book was ever made into a movie, but it should have been. I imagine a movie version looking and feeling a lot like the 1974 version of *The Great Gatsby*, the cinema portrayal of F. Scott Fitzgerald's classic novel of the same name. Written by Francis Ford Coppola and directed by Jack Clayton, this version of *Gatsby* starred Robert Redford as Jay Gatsby and Mia Farrow as Daisy Buchanan. I've always felt that the movie captured the same mood of quiet desperation that permeated the between-the-lines level of the novel.

It seems to me that when as a trader you lose big, you want to get back in the market right away to make it back, while after a big win you feel like taking time off to appreciate the glow of victory. After one huge win Livermore bought a yacht and took a long European cruise. This is probably wrongheaded psychology, because you win when you are in concert with the markets and this is exactly the time when you should stay invested. You lose when things are going against you and this is precisely when you should step aside. I wonder what Jesse Livermore would say. How about this quote attributed to him? "There are only two emotions in the market, hope and fear—the only problem is you hope when you should fear and you fear when you should hope."

Currently, my thesis on the big picture is simple: *The only answer to overwhelming debt is inflation.*

I have been investing by this thesis, but it has not always gone my way. I have been trying to hang tough. As Livermore once recommended, "The big money is made sitting, not thinking. Men who can both be right and sit tight are uncommon." But by the middle of 2012, I had had a rough time of it—inflation remained low and I had taken significant losses in the precious-metals trade. I still believe that the tremendous borrowing currently being done by governments around the world will soon produce inflation and the appreciation of hard assets like gold and real estate. This borrowing will continue because stimulated growth and trailing inflation is the only way these countries will ever be able to pay back their debts.

Take a typical family as an example. A few years ago they had two good incomes coming in—say, $15,000 per month or $180,000 per year. After taxes in the 35 percent bracket they had $9,750 per month left to live on. But—wait a minute—they realized that they could borrow money to buy a big house with a big monthly mortgage of, say, $8,000 per month, because after the mortgage interest deduction on their taxes they saved 35 percent of the monthly mortgage payment ($2,800 per month). The amount of principal paid down is so low in the early years of a mortgage that it is insignificant here. So they bought the big house and their net cost after taxes was about $5,200 per month. This was only 34.7 percent of their income. *No problem, eh?*

So after five years of economic quicksand the family is left with only one of the incomes—the big one—so they only have $8,000 coming in each month. The mortgage still takes $8,000, but since they are making less money, the mortgage interest deduction is probably only 25 percent of their new income of $8,000 per month ($2,000). They are making less and have dropped into a lower tax bracket; the deduction is a smaller percentage of a smaller income. Their new bottom-line cost for the house becomes about $6,000 per month—*$800 more than when they were doing well.* So goes the downward spiral.

But how do the numbers work out if there is an environment of controlled but significant inflation? Let's say the inflation rate is an uncomfortable 5 percent. After five years, the time we have been in this mess so far, and assuming that both wages and prices were in the upward inflationary trend, the numbers would work out something like in the table below.

It is clear that it will be much easier for the family to manage their debt once inflation has reduced the impact of *the very same mortgage payment* to about 47 percent of their income versus 75 percent before the inflation.

Impact of Inflation on Mortgage Affordability

YEAR	INCOME	DEDUCT	NET MORT	PERCENT OF INCOME
1	$8,000	$2,000*	$6,000	75 percent
2	$8,400	$2,100*	$5,900	70 percent
3	$8,820	$2,646**	$5,354	61 percent
4	$9,261	$2,778**	$5,222	56 percent
5	$9,724	$3,403***	$4,597	47 percent

*25 percent Tax Bracket; **30 percent Tax Bracket; ***35 percent Tax Bracket

This is a deliberate worst-case example, and the tax bracket break points are arbitrary, but the concept is true.

I believe the very same thing is true of the titanic levels of global debt. Inflation is not only the best answer; it has been shown historically that *it is the only answer*. Remember how they inflated the Vietnam War debt away in the late 1970s? That is why my big-picture global thesis is inflation even though by the end of 2013 deflation was still stalking the markets.

So now that I have decided that inflation is ahead, how do I invest? I would say gold, oil, any hard asset. One guy on "the Street" is famous for putting it this way: "I only want to buy stuff that would hurt like hell if I dropped it on my foot." Oddly enough, during periods of high inflation you want to have as much borrowed money (fixed rate) as possible. See the table above for the reason.

Fine, I want gold. But if there is a lot of inflation in America, won't the dollar-value of the gold diminish compared to countries with low inflation, like those who mine the hard assets we want? Maybe. To be sure that this currency effect does not mess up our trade, I think I want to buy my gold in Canadian dollars. Also, a little dividend couldn't hurt. So that brings me to Agnico-Eagle Mines (AEM), a Canadian gold mining company with a small dividend. This is how I saw it in 2010, when I bought AEM for $60.17 in March and sold it for $71.33 in October for a profit of $11.16 per share. When everything else went bad in the summer of 2010, AEM was the bulwark that kept me afloat. I also traded Gold Corp (GG), but this foreign miner came with foreign taxes too; this offset any possible currency benefit.

Then, after the market correction in 2010 and early 2011, I again looked to gold and AEM. I bought AEM again on August 2, 2011, for $58, as I repopulated my dividend portfolio, and immediately sold covered calls against it. The volatility of gold makes this trade work well. When gold came down, I bought back the AEM calls I had sold for a profit. The stock moved up nicely toward the end of the month; the price of gold was increasing with the fears there would be another attack on the ten-year anniversary of the 9/11 terrorist attacks. AEM peaked at $71.67 on the Friday before the anniversary. When gold moved back up, I sold some more covered calls against my AEM stock. I used this strategy for three round trips, bringing my cost basis for the stock down by $5.46 through option hedging alone.

So the net cost for the AEM position I held at the beginning of September 2011, including the three round trips of covered calls and the two trips owning the stock, was $41.38 per share. There were also two dividend payments of $0.15 each during the time I owned the stock and after receiving the $0.30 my cost basis dropped to $41.08 per share. This was fortunate because the price of gold was going to correct in early 2012 and AEM stock started a long trend downward as the price of gold also faltered. The important thing is that the covered call hedging strategy I used in 2011 reduced my loss from about 10 percent to about 5 percent while the stock dropped over 39 percent from my second buy price. Unfortunately for me, I was preoccupied with getting a novel out and didn't take profits when AEM hit what seems like a hard resistance level at just above $71. Added to my distraction was a bout of greed; I got greedy while shopping for more calls to sell, and this led to my getting caught without the protection I needed during the next downturn in gold.

The $5.46 in hedging money reduced the cost basis of the second trip into AEM stock from $58 to $52.54. The trade didn't start losing money until the stock dropped below this new cost basis. When the first round trip in and out of the stock is included, the trade was good above $41.08. As often happens, AEM came back up after I finally closed out the trade, and by July 3, 2012, it was back to trading at $42.54, up over $7 from where I sold it. I was vindicated; however, by June 2013 both AEM and GG traded down to $25.

Trading Around My AEM Position

SECURITY	BUY PRICE ($)	SELL PRICE ($)	TRADE GAIN/ LOSS ($)	TRADE GAIN/ LOSS (%)	TOTAL AT RISK ($)	NET RETURN ($)	NET RETURN (%)
AEM	60.17	71.33	+11.16	+18.6	60.17	+11.16	18.6
AEM	58.00	35.25	-22.75	-20.0	118.17	-11.59	-9.8
Sep 67.50C	1.22	2.01	+0.79	+100	120.18	-10.08	-8.4
Nov 70.00C	0.48	2.55	+2.07	+100	122.73	-8.73	-7.1
Jan 67.50C	Expired	2.60	+2.60	+100	125.33	-6.13	-4.9
Dividend	—	0.30	+0.30	+100	125.33	+5.83	-4.7

Remember, the calls are sold before they are bought! If you do not own the underlying stock, the downside potential of selling naked calls is *infinite*! If you don't own the stock on expiration day, you will need to buy it in order to honor the contract to provide the stock—at whatever the selling price is on that day. Since it is mathematically possible that the stock goes up forever, there is no cap to losses. Selling naked calls is not for me.

As long as the markets remain volatile, the use of covered calls and collars continues making profit; just as important, if the markets become range bound these structures keep making yield to live on while you wait. The Volatility Index (VIX) was over 30 for months in 2010—much higher than the historical average of around 20, but much lower than the stratospheric levels seen during the height of the crash in December 2008 when it breached 70. (The VIX spiked to 150 during the 1987 crash.) Getting a little return while waiting is nice, but the process does so much more; it takes down your risk while providing predictable potential upside.

The other possibility of the trade is the stock price moves up and goes beyond the strike price of the last call sold; in this event the underlying stock will be called away—that is, your broker will sell the stock at the strike price automatically. The upside potential is capped by the call strike price. The last one I sold was at $67.50, but this would still have generated a very good profit had the stock been called away at $67.50. The profit in the stock, when called away, would have been $9.50, the hedging profit would have been $5.46, and the dividends paid would have equaled $0.30. In that eventuality the total profit on the original $58.00 invested would have been $15.26, or 26.3 percent in just a few months, with downside risk controlled and the stock moribund.

My AEM trade was great right up to the point at which I ignored the signals, when the Gold ETF (GLD) broke down and penetrated the two-hundred-day average. At this point it would have taken a huge amount of hedging to protect the stock from the 45 percent shellacking it finally took. Better to listen to what the market is saying and sell outright when the signal comes. I saw the break in the gold market, noting in my trading log that GLD had broken below its two-hundred-day moving average. That was when the price really started to break down, but I couldn't bring myself to believe that my long-term thesis was wrong and I should again trade out of the stock. By the end of 2011, AEM had dropped to $36.23. I held on until March 2012, when I closed out the AEM position at $35.35, for a net loss on all my AEM trades of $5.73. Bad enough when considering how poorly I handled the break in gold, but much less than it could have been without hedging.

> **Lesson:** *Listen to the market. It will tell you all the insider information you will ever need if you will just listen.*

Howling at the Moon

There is one more thing about personal opinion, politics, trading, and life. I was born in the middle of the Mojave Desert. There is a culture in the desert that is impossible for people who are not raised there to understand. Desert people are very proud and very stubborn. We are opinionated and passionate. But, above all, we are practical; we must be to make a go of it there. In the best parts of the desert, in the parts with just a little water, lives one of my favorite desert animals: the coyote. The coyote has an odd habit of howling at the moon. It is not practical for the coyote to waste energy doing this; it doesn't change the moon or the hard life the coyote lives. But being a coyote, he does it anyway. It is not very practical for an investor to imitate the coyote.

Shortly after the worst of the 2008 crash had passed, I met a guy at my neighborhood bar. He is from eastern Europe, but he has been here since 1985—long enough to have experienced his second market crash and plenty of earthquakes. Once a newcomer experiences a 6.0 quake or larger, he automatically becomes a native Californian; living through two crashes makes him a conservative investor. We had a long conversation about the state of the economy. He went on and on about the inequities of the system. He bashed the bankers for long tedious minutes. He listed the CEOs who ran their companies into the ground while they made tens of millions of dollars in bonuses. He complained that our representatives in the government were all out for themselves. He howled and howled.

He was right, of course, and I told him so. I told him that he was exactly correct in his accusations and his descriptions of the way the banking system operates. I told him over and over that he was right, that he had it exactly correct. Yes, the rich bankers and CEOs did make a lot of money while the companies for which they were responsible tanked. Yes, it sucked. But it was all irrelevant. I told him that I was a trader, a flea, and that I needed to emotionlessly evaluate the environment and trade accordingly.

I met another howler recently—much more pleasant, but a howler nonetheless. I was at the dentist's office for a cleaning, and while I waited in the quiet anteroom with the receptionist, I tried to sell her a copy of my last novel, *Carnival of Cannibals*. She declined, saying, "I rarely read fiction. I usually read nonfiction." Oh? So I immediately tacked the conversation to my new book, this one, on trading. I didn't recognize right away that the receptionist had become bitter about the markets and stocks, so I told her my new book was nonfiction about trading the stock market—specifically, the options market—and that I would bring her a copy once it was published.

To my great surprise she immediately became animated, if not angry, and began complaining about the price of gasoline. So I tried to explain how I use oil industry investments to protect me from the variability in the price of oil and gas; my trades of Kinder Morgan Partners more than paid for the recent increases in the price of gas, in fact they paid the car loan too. Then she really got going, saying she didn't want to make money from speculation—too many people are hurt by the high price of gas.

Uh-oh. I didn't see that coming.

When I asked if she had a 401(k) or other investments she told me she did, but that her husband made all the decisions. All right, I would bring a copy for her husband. But it was no use; I was evil for having anything to do with the stock market. What did I have to lose? I told her that I thought her argument was internally conflicted—either she wanted her investments to make money or she should not invest. I always start an investment discussion under the assumption that an investor actually wants to make money.

I was reminded of a quote from Edwin Lefèvre's *Reminiscences of a Stock Operator*: "It does not take a reasonably young and normal man very long to lose the habit of being poor. It requires a little longer to forget that he used to be rich." Maybe my dentist's receptionist and her husband just lost too much in 2008 and maybe they had been hit hard in 2001 as well. During the last ten or twelve years, if you were not short-term trading, you inevitably took a big hit. I can understand how people can be bitter.

As traders, as investors, it's fine to complain about how the system is stacked against the little guy, but does that help us build wealth? Wealth creation takes time, so we need to get started as soon as pos-sible. Standing on the sidelines because the system is fixed won't get us to our goal.

I am a capitalist; I do not apologize for this. But I don't have infinite capital; I need to be right more than I am wrong. Every cent of income I receive comes from the application of capital. I can't wait for the markets to once again go up in a steady, bullish fashion to invest, and I think any-one who has retirement on their mind had better not wait either. I told my complaining friend in the bar that whining about the inequities of the sys-tem was like a coyote howling at the moon: not only does it not improve the situation, it is a huge waste of time and energy. As the saying goes, "If you can't beat 'em, join 'em." And if you can't bring yourself to join them, you at least need to trade with them. We can't wait for the markets and our government to start behaving rationally once again. We need to trade, as the markets stabilize our trading will evolve into investing.

Useful Stuff

Handy Exchange Traded Funds (ETFs) and Real Estate Investment Trusts (REITs)

The following list is by no means a complete one. There are hundreds of ETFs now, long or short almost anything. Some of these are very thinly traded and some have two-time or three-time leverage. These are just some I have used in the past. Be sure that you understand exactly what an ETF tracks and how it is managed before you invest in it.

Short ETFs

QID—Short the QQQ, the NASDAQ Composite
DOG—Short the Dow 30 Industrial Average
SDS—Short the S&P 500 Average
FXP—Short China
SRS—Ultrashort real estate
SKF—Ultrashort financials
PST—Ultrashort seven- to ten-year Treasuries

TBT—Ultrashort twenty-year Treasuries

TBF—Short twenty-year Treasuries

TBX—Short seven- to ten-year Treasuries

DTYS—Short ten-year Treasuries

DTUS—Short two-year Treasuries

Long ETFs

USO—Long oil

BPZ—Long oil

UNG—Long natural gas

KOL—Long coal

GLD—Long gold

DGB—Ultralong gold (two times)

DBA—Long soft commodities

XLB—Long materials

UYM—Ultralong basic materials

XLP—Long consumer staples

XLY—Long consumer discretionary sector

XLV—Long health care

MOO—Long agriculture

DBA—Long grain futures

XLF—Long financials

UYG—Ultralong financials (two times)

FAS—Ultra-ultralong financials (three times)

KRE—Long regional banks

XHB—Long home builders

TLT—Long twenty-year Treasuries

TIP—Long twenty-year Treasury TIPs

IYT—Long Dow Transport Index

BZF—Long Brazil

EWZ—Long Brazil

FXI—Long China, Xinhua Average

HAO—Long China, small cap stocks

EWH—Long Hong Kong stocks
CYB—Long Chinese currency
RDX—Long Russia
PIN—Long India
EPI—Long India
EZA—Long South Africa
EWA—Long Australia
EWT—Long Taiwan
ECH—Long Chile
EWM—Long Malaysia

Long REITs

NLY—Annaly Capital Management, Inc.
AGNC—American Capital Agency Corp.
CIM—Chimera Investment Corp.
LAND.L—Land Securities Group plc
HMSO.L—Hammerson plc
DLN.L—Dewent London plc
SHB.L—Shaftesbury plc
GPOR.L—Great Portland Estates plc
MFA—MFA Financial, Inc.
CMO—Capstead Mortgage Corp.
ANH—Anworth Mortgage Corp.

Brokerage House Contact Information

Charles Schwab Corp.
  211 Main Street
  San Francisco, CA 94105
  Contact numbers: (415) 636-7000 or (800) 648-5300

TD Ameritrade Corp., a subsidiary of Toronto Dominion Bank
  P.O. Box 2760
  Omaha, NE 68103
  Contact numbers: (800) 454-9272 or (800) 669-3900

Scottrade Inc.
  12800 Corporate Hill Road
  St. Louis, MO 63131
  Contact numbers: (314) 965-1555 or (800) 619-7283

Merrill Lynch, a subsidiary of Bank of America
  1400 Merrill Lynch Drive
  Pennington, NJ 08534
  Contact numbers: (800) 228-4015 or (877) 902-8730

E*Trade Financial Corp.
  11713 Gorham Avenue
  Los Angeles, CA 90049
  Contact number: (800) 786-2575

Precious Metals Dealer Contact Information

American Century Investments
P.O. Box 419200
Kansas City, MO 64111
Contact number: (888) 345-2071

FideliTrade Inc.
3601 N. Market Street
Wilmington, DE 19802
Contact number: (800) 223-1080

Dillon Gage Inc.
15301 Dallas Parkway, Ste. 200
Addison, TX 75001
Contact number: (800) 375-4653

Rare Coins of New Hampshire
28 Jones Road, Ste. 1
P.O. Box 720
Milford, NH 03055
Contact number: (800) 225-7264

Manfra, Tordella & Brooks Inc.
90 Broad Street
New York, NY 10004
Contact number: (800) 535-7481

Bollinger Bands and Statistical Process Control –

Technitrader.com explanation of Bollinger Bands
...the market trends sideways 60-70% of the time. Using Bollinger Bands can help you find breakout patterns, entry set-ups, and low-risk trades. Bollinger Bands are easy to use and interpret. Many traders who struggle to read candlestick charts and trend patterns find Bollinger Bands a huge help in analyzing stock charts.

Bollinger Bands work in certain Market Conditions and can give false exit signals if used in the wrong Market Conditions. It is imperative that if you decide to use Bollinger Bands that you understand when to use them and when they will give you false signals. The last thing you want to do is exit a trade only to watch it run and run while you are not in it. This happens often to traders who do not understand the proper use of Bollinger Bands or other channel indicators.

Bollinger Bands are the best channel indicator because of their unique ability to contract or expand. But as with all channel indicators they are designed for specific types of price action and market conditions. A Velocity Market Condition, as an example is not ideal for Bollinger Band use. Instead you should use the leading hybrid velocity indicators designed for this fast accelerating price action.

Bollinger Bands are a one of a kind channel indicator that helps improve your trading while reducing the complexity of searching for great picks. Understanding leading indicators will allow you to trade stocks with greater success than just following prevailing trader action in the market.

Bollinger Bands were written by John Bollinger and are a derivative of envelope channels. They perform better than standard channels. The concept of a channel, or two lines that surround price action, in stocks is that you will better be able to see overbought and oversold conditions. Also for traders who struggle to see trend line patterns and the angle of trend, Bollinger Bands can help.

Bollinger Bands can help you develop Spatial Pattern Recognitions Skills which are essential in trading today's electronic and technically driven marketplace.

Wikipedia Article on Statistical Process Control

Statistical Process Control is a method of quality control which uses statistical methods. SPC is applied in order to monitor and control a process. Monitoring and controlling the process ensures that it operates at its full potential. At its full potential, the process can make as much conforming product as possible with a minimum (if not an elimination) of waste. SPC can be applied to any process where the "conforming product" (product meeting specifications) output can be measured. Some key tools are used in SPC. These include control charts a focus on continuous improvement; and the design of experiments. An example of a process where SPC is applied is manufacturing lines.

SPC was pioneered by Walter A. Shewhart in the early 1920s. W. Edwards Deming later applied SPC methods in the United States during World War II, to improve quality in the manufacture of munitions and other strategically important products. Deming was also instrumental in introducing SPC methods to Japanese industry after the war had ended. Shewhart developed the "control chart" and the concept of a state of statistical control determined by carefully designed experiments.

While Shewhart drew from pure mathematical statistical theories, he understood that data from physical processes seldom produced a "normal distribution curve"; that is, a Gaussian distribution or bell curve. He discovered that data from measurements of variation in manufacturing did not always behave the same way as did data from measurements of natural phenomena (for example, Brownian motion of particles). Shewhart concluded that while every process displays variation, some processes display variation that is controlled and natural to the process ("common" sources of variation). Other processes display variation that is not controlled and that is not present in the causal system of the process at all times ("special" sources of variation).

Control charts – The data from measurements of variations at points on the process map is monitored using control charts. Control charts can differentiate "assignable" ("special") sources of variation from "common" sources. "Common" sources, because they are an expected part of the process, are of much less concern to the manufacturer than "assignable" sources. Using control charts is a continuous activity, ongoing over time.

Stable process – When the process does not trigger any of the control chart "detection rules" for the control chart, it is said to be "stable". A process capability analysis may be performed on a stable process to predict the ability of the process to produce "conforming product" in the future.

Excessive variation – When the process triggers any of the control chart "detection rules", (or alternatively, the process capability is low), other activities may be performed to identify the source of the excessive variation. The tools used in these extra activities include: Ishikawa diagrams, designed experiments and Pareto charts. Designed experiments are critical to this phase of the application of SPC. They are the only means of objectively quantifying the relative importance (strength) of sources of variation. Once the sources of variation have been quantified, those sources that are both statistically and practically significant can be eliminated. (A source that is statistically significant may not be considered cost effective to eliminate. A source that is not statistically significant would not be considered significant in practical terms). Methods of eliminating a source of variation might include: development of standards; staff training; error-proofing and changes to the process itself.

Six Sigma is a, business management strategy, originally developed by Motorola in 1986. Six Sigma became well known after Jack Welch made it a central focus of his business strategy at General Electric in 1995, and today it is widely used in many sectors of industry.

The term *Six Sigma* originated from terminology associated with manufacturing, specifically terms associated with statistical modeling of manufacturing processes. The maturity of a manufacturing process can be described by a *sigma* rating indicating its yield, or the percentage of defect-free products it creates. A six sigma process is one in which 99.99966% of the products manufactured are statistically expected to be free of defects (3.4 defects per million). Motorola set a goal of "six sigma" for all its manufacturing operations, and this goal became a byword for the management and engineering practices used to achieve it.

Six Sigma originated as a set of practices designed to improve manufacturing processes and eliminate defects, but its application was subsequently extended to other types of business processes as well. In Six Sigma, a defect is defined as any process output that does not meet customer specifications, or that could lead to creating an output that does not meet customer specifications.

Like its predecessors, Six Sigma doctrine asserts that:

- Continuous efforts to achieve stable and predictable process results (i.e., reduce process variation) are of vital importance to business success.

- Manufacturing and business processes have characteristics that can be measured, analyzed, improved and controlled.

- Achieving sustained quality improvement requires commitment from the entire organization, particularly from top-level management.

Features that set Six Sigma apart from previous quality improvement initiatives include:

- A clear focus on achieving measurable and quantifiable financial returns from any Six Sigma project.

- An increased emphasis on strong and passionate management leadership and support.

- A special infrastructure of "Champions", "Master Black Belts", "Black Belts", "Green Belts", "Red Belts" etc. to lead and implement the Six Sigma approach.

- A clear commitment to making decisions on the basis of verifiable data, rather than assumptions and guesswork.

The term "Six Sigma" comes from a field of statistics known as process capability studies. Originally, it referred to the ability of manufacturing processes to produce a very high proportion of output within specification. Processes that operate with "six sigma quality" over the short term are assumed to produce long-term defect levels below 3.4 defects per million opportunities (DPMO). Six Sigma's implicit goal is to improve all processes to that level of quality or better.

Origin and meaning of the term "six sigma process" – The term "six sigma process" comes from the notion that if one has six standard deviations between the process mean and the nearest specification limit, as shown in the graph, practically no items will fail to meet specifications. This is based on the calculation method employed in process capability studies.

Capability studies measure the number of standard deviations between the process mean and the nearest specification limit in sigma units. As process standard deviation goes up, or the mean of the process

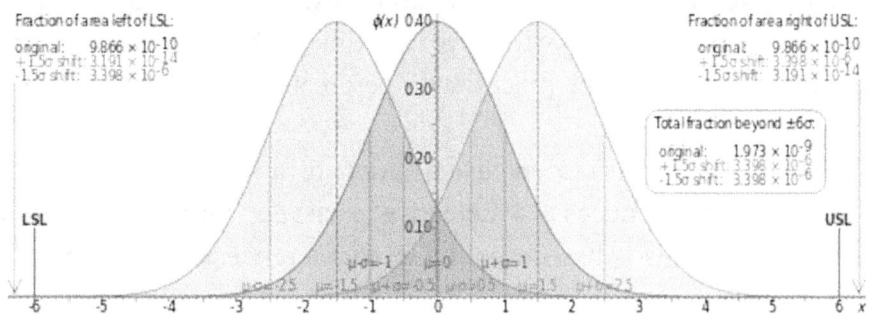

moves away from the center of the tolerance, fewer standard deviations will fit between the mean and the nearest specification limit, decreasing the sigma number and increasing the likelihood of items outside specification.

Graph of the normal distribution, which underlies the statistical assumptions of the Six Sigma model. The Greek letter σ (sigma) marks the distance on the horizontal axis between the mean, μ, and the curve's inflection point. The greater this distance, the greater is the spread of values encountered. For the green curve shown above, μ = 0 and σ = 1. The upper and lower specification limits (USL and LSL, respectively) are at a distance of 6σ from the mean. Because of the properties of the normal distribution, values lying that far away from the mean are extremely unlikely. Even if the mean were to move right or left by 1.5σ at some point in the future (1.5 sigma shift, colored red and blue), there is still a good safety cushion. This is why Six Sigma aims to have processes where the mean is at least 6σ away from the nearest specification limit.

Role of the 1.5 sigma shift – Experience has shown that processes usually do not perform as well in the long term as they do in the short term. As a result, the number of sigmas that will fit between the process mean and the nearest specification limit may well drop over time, compared to an initial short-term study. To account for this real-life increase in process variation over time, an empirically-based 1.5 sigma shift is introduced into the calculation. According to this idea, a process that fits 6 sigma between the process mean and the nearest specification limit in a short-term study will in the long term fit only 4.5 sigma – either because the process mean will move over time, or because the long-term standard deviation of the process will be greater than that observed in the short term, or both.

Hence the widely accepted definition of a six sigma process is a process that produces 3.4 defective parts per million opportunities (DPMO). This is based on the fact that a process that is normally distributed will have 3.4 parts per million beyond a point that is 4.5 standard deviations above or below the mean (one-sided capability study). So the 3.4 DPMO of a six sigma process in fact corresponds to 4.5 sigma, namely 6 sigma minus the 1.5-sigma shift introduced to account for long-term variation. This allows for the fact that special causes may result in a deterioration in process performance over time, and is designed to prevent underestimation of the defect levels likely to be encountered in real-life operation.

Sigma levels

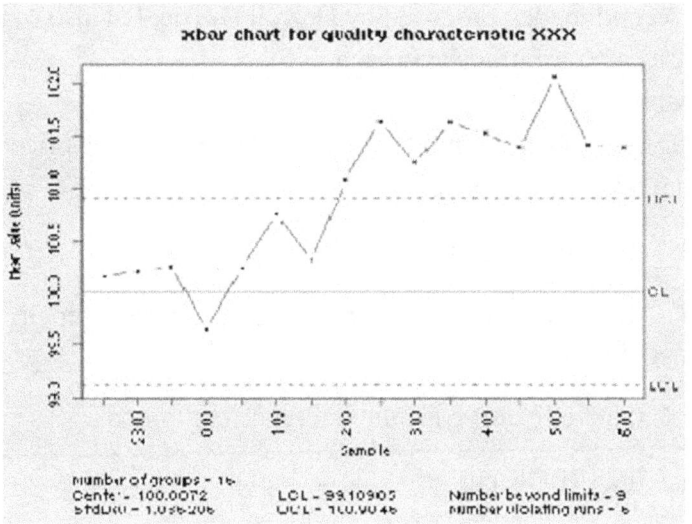

A control chart depicting a process that experienced a 1.5 sigma drift in the process mean toward the upper specification limit starting at midnight. Control charts are used to maintain 6 sigma quality by signaling when quality professionals should investigate a process to find and eliminate special-cause variation.

See also: Three sigma rule.

Wikipedia Entry on Credit Default Swap Pricing

Pricing and valuation

There are two competing theories usually advanced for the pricing of credit default swaps. The first, which for convenience we will refer to as the 'probability model', takes the present value of a series of cash flows weighted by their probability of non-default. This method suggests that credit default swaps should trade at a considerably lower spread than corporate bonds.

The second model, proposed by Darrell Duffie, but also by Hull and White, uses a no-arbitrage approach.

Probability model

Under the probability model, a credit default swap is priced using a model that takes four inputs:

- the issue premium,

- the recovery rate (percentage of notional repaid in event of default),

- the credit curve for the reference entity and

- the LIBOR curve.

If default events never occurred the price of a CDS would simply be the sum of the discounted premium payments. So CDS pricing models have to take into account the possibility of a default occurring some time between the effective date and maturity date of the CDS contract. For the purpose of explanation we can imagine the case of a one year CDS with effective date t_0 with four quarterly premium payments occurring at times t_1, t_2, t_3, and t_4. If the nominal for the CDS is N and the issue premium is c then the size of the quarterly premium payments is $Nc / 4$.

If we assume for simplicity that defaults can only occur on one of the payment dates then there are five ways the contract could end: either it does not have any default at all, so the four premium payments are made and the contract survives until the maturity date, or a default occurs on the first, second, third or fourth payment date. To price the CDS we now need to assign probabilities to the five possible outcomes, then calculate the present value of the payoff for each outcome. The present value of the CDS is then simply the <u>present value</u> of the five payoffs multiplied by their probability of occurring.

This is illustrated in the following tree diagram where at each payment date either the contract has a default event, in which case it ends with a payment of $N(1 - R)$ shown in red, where R is the recovery rate, or it survives without a default being triggered, in which case a premium payment of $Nc / 4$ is made, shown in blue. At either side of the diagram are the cashflows up to that point in time with premium payments in blue and default payments in red. If the contract is terminated the square is shown with solid shading.

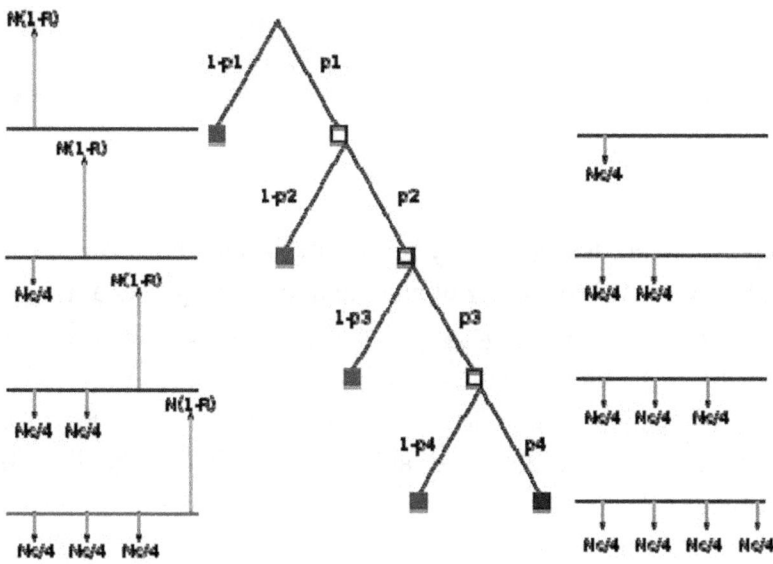

The probability of surviving over the interval t_{i-1} to t_i without a default payment is p_i and the probability of a default being triggered is $1 - p_i$. The calculation of present value, given <u>discount factors</u> of δ_1 to δ_4 is then

Description	Premium Payment PV	Default Payment PV	Probability
Default at time t_1	0	$N(1 - R)\delta_1$	$1 - p_1$
Default at time t_2	$-\dfrac{Nc}{4}\delta_1$	$N(1 - R)\delta_2$	$p_1(1 - p_2)$
Default at time t_3	$-\dfrac{Nc}{4}(\delta_1 + \delta_2)$	$N(1 - R)\delta_3$	$p_1 p_2 (1 - p_3)$
Default at time t_4	$-\dfrac{Nc}{4}(\delta_1 + \delta_2 + \delta_3)$	$N(1 - R)\delta_4$	$p_1 p_2 p_3 (1 - p_4)$
No defaults	$-\dfrac{Nc}{4}(\delta_1 + \delta_2 + \delta_3 + \delta_4)$	0	$p_1 \times p_2 \times p_3 \times p_4$

The probabilities p_1, p_2, p_3, p_4 can be calculated using the <u>credit spread</u> curve. The probability of no default occurring over a time period from t to $t + \Delta t$ <u>decays exponentially</u> with a time-constant determined by the credit spread, or mathematically $p = exp(-s(t)\Delta t)$ where $s(t)$ is the <u>credit spread</u> zero curve at time t. The riskier the reference entity the greater the spread and the more rapidly the survival probability decays with time.

To get the total present value of the credit default swap we multiply the probability of each outcome by its present value to give

$$PV = (1 - p_1)N(1 - R)\delta_1$$
$$+ p_1(1 - p_2)[N(1 - R)\delta_2 - \frac{Nc}{4}\delta_1]$$
$$+ p_1 p_2(1 - p_3)[N(1 - R)\delta_3 - \frac{Nc}{4}(\delta_1 + \delta_2)]$$
$$+ p_1 p_2 p_3(1 - p_4)[N(1 - R)\delta_4 - \frac{Nc}{4}(\delta_1 + \delta_2 + \delta_3)]$$
$$- p_1 p_2 p_3 p_4(\delta_1 + \delta_2 + \delta_3 + \delta_4)\frac{Nc}{4}$$

No-arbitrage model

In the 'no-arbitrage' model proposed by both Duffie, and Hull and White, it is assumed that there is no risk free arbitrage. Duffie uses the LIBOR as the risk free rate, whereas Hull and White use US Treasuries as the risk free rate. Both analyses make simplifying assumptions (such as the assumption that there is zero cost of unwinding the fixed leg of the swap on default), which may invalidate the no-arbitrage assumption. However the Duffie approach is frequently used by the market to determine theoretical prices. Under the Duffie construct, the price of a credit default swap can also be derived by calculating the asset swap spread of a bond. If a bond has a spread of 100, and the swap spread is 70 basis points, then a CDS contract should trade at 30. However there are sometimes technical reasons why this will not be the case, and this may or may not present an arbitrage opportunity for the canny investor. The difference between the theoretical model and the actual price of a credit default swap is known as the basis.

Bibliography

American Bar Association. *Guide to Wills & Estates*. 2nd ed. New York: Random House, 2004.

Barofsky, Neil. *Bailout: An Inside Account of How Washington Abandoned Main Street while Rescuing Wall Street*. New York: Simon & Schuster, 2012.

Brown, Constance. *Technical Analysis Demystified*. New York: McGraw-Hill, 2008.

Burdick, Donald L., and William L. Leffler. *Petrochemicals in Nontechnical Language*. 3rd ed. Tulsa, OK: PennWell, 2001.

Churchill, Winston S. *The Birth of Britain*. New York: Bantam, 1956.

Cobleigh, Ira U., and Bruce K. Dorfman. *The Roaring Eighties on Wall Street*. New York: Macmillian, 1981.

Cramer, James J. *Confessions of a Street Addict*. New York: Simon & Schuster, 2002.

Cramer, James J., with Cliff Mason. *Getting Back to Even*. New York: Simon & Schuster, 2009.

Frost, A. J., and Robert R. Prechter. *Elliott Wave Principle*. 20th anniv. ed. Chichester, West Sussex, England: John Wiley & Sons, 1999.

Gardner, David, and Tom Gardner. *The Motley Fool Million Dollar Portfolio: How to Build and Grow a Panic-Proof Investment Portfolio.* New York: HarperCollins, 2009.

James, Lawrence. *The Rise and Fall of the British Empire.* New York: St. Martin's, 1994.

Langemeier, Loral. *The Millionaire Maker: Act, Think, and Make Money the Way the Wealthy Do.* New York: McGraw-Hill, 2006.

Lefèvre, Edwin. *Reminiscences of a Stock Operator.* Hoboken, NJ: John Wiley & Sons, 2005.

Leffler, William L. *Petroleum Refining in Non Technical Language.* 3rd ed. Tulsa, OK: PennWell, 2000.

Lucia, Raymond J., with Dale Fetherling. *Buckets of Money: How to Retire in Comfort and Safety.* Hoboken, NJ: John Wiley & Sons, 2004.

Lucia, Raymond J., with Dale Fetherling. *Retire!* Carlsbad, CA: New Beginnings, 2007.

McMillan, Lawrence G. *Options As a Strategic Investment.* New York: Simon & Schuster, 1986.

Nassar, David S. *Rules of the Trade.* New York: McGraw-Hill, 2001.

O'Connel, Robert L. *The Ghosts of Cannae.* New York: Random House, 2010.

Prechter, Robert R., Jr. *Conquer the Crash: You Can Survive and Prosper in a Deflationary Depression.* Hoboken, NJ: John Wiley & Sons, 2002.

Richelson, Hildy, and Stan Richelson. *Bonds, The Unbeaten Path to Secure Investment Growth.* New York: Bloomberg, 2007.

Silverstein, Jim. *Movie Quotes to Get You through Life.* 3rd ed. N.p.: Jim Silverstein, 2010.

Sorkin, Andrew Ross. *Too Big to Fail: The Inside Story of How Wall Street and Washington Fought to Save the Financial System—and Themselves.* New York: Penguin, 2009.

Stern, W. Rod. *Estate Planning, Wills and Trusts: For Business Owners and Entrepreneurs.* Irvine, CA: Entrepreneur Media, 2007.

Turk, James, and John Rubino. *The Collapse of the Dollar.* New York: Doubleday, 2004.

www.ingramcontent.com/pod-product-compliance
Lightning Source LLC
Chambersburg PA
CBHW071408170526
45165CB00001B/215